MW00576255

shelter of the sacred

poetry from

2016 and 2017

red thread letters

from

shiloh sophia

shelter of the sacred

Poetry from 2016-2017

Copyright © 2018 by Shiloh Sophia McCloud

Published by Cosmic Cowgirls Ink, LLC

Cover art: Shelter of the Sacred by Shiloh Sophia, 2017
Author photo by Lloyd Johnson

Printed in the United Sates of America

These poems love to be shared with proper author credit.

ISBN: 978-0-9674214-3-8

table of contents

And all shall be well and
All manner of thing shall be well
When the tongues of flames are in-folded
Into the crowned knot of fire
And the fire and the rose are one.
~T.S. Eliot~

Instead of thinking of what to do before you die -
think of what to do that makes you come alive!!
Do that instead.
~ Shiloh Sophia ~

"I have not a clue whether we humans
will live for another 100 or 10,000 years.
We can't be sure.
What matters to me is the fact we have fallen out
of a very ancient love affair – a kind of dream tangle,
with the earth itself.
If, through our own mess, that relationship is about to end,
then we need to scatter as much beauty around us
as we possibly can, to send a voice,
to attempt some kind of repair.
I think of it as a kind of courting – a very old idea.
This isn't about statistical hysteria, it's about personal style.
Any other response is just not cool".
~ Dr. Martin Shaw ~

red Thread letter from the author

Dear One,

*I can't tell you how grateful I am that you are here. Really here
where I am and really there where you are. Thank you for
showing up.*

This offering of words was written in the early morning
with candles, tea and often, kittens. Words that gave me
something to do with all the love I felt in my heart for
you, for our people, and for the future of the planet. The
poems in the Shelter of the Sacred were written over two
years 2016-2017 and shared in Red Thread Letters that I
write for my community. As I went back through the
tangle of tragedy, the bounty of breakthrough, the rebel
prayers and the singing of blessings, I was interested
how much of my work was in response to suffering. This
idea, to do my part to alleviate suffering, has been with
me for as long as I can remember; that I could make it
easier for others through some kind offering. But what?

For me, mostly it is through painting and writing.
Through choosing not to turn away from suffering and
instead, give those within my circles tools to turn
towards it. And yes, I do believe and know, that painting

2

and poetry are indeed part of the medicine to guide us into resilience. Resilience and rebellion seem to be the bookends of my pilgrimage here on earth.

My piece of the red thread, that which is mine to hold, is woven into these pages. Some are threads of blood red soaked with violence. Others are joyfully magenta with invitation to come to play. Many threads are scarlet-hued; stained by the sunset of my home in Sonoma. And there are the purple ones too, those that are mingled with grief and groaning. There are ones that are hot pink, made of lace for my lover. Then there are the true red ones. Those threads are an invitation to your own waking up journey. A few poems may have snuck into Tea with the Midnight Muse, yet I wanted to offer this in its entirety of two years of early mornings.

Ever since I was a child I had the feeling that something was wrong, missing - or being withheld. I had moments as a punk teenager of thinking we were all under a spell. Of course, I rebelled. What else does one do when one begins to gain awareness - and notices that the systems and histories set up all around them are somehow designed to enforce another agenda than the one that is natural to being human?

3

At some level I believe I made a choice as a very young woman to fight the establishment. How I thought I would do that and how I do that now is a story for another day. I would however like to tell you the story of what I DID discover after 25 years.

One of my earliest potent poems from when I was 12-ish was called -"Something is Not Right." I remember sitting in my room, writing it and discovering that as I wrote it, I was getting information in the moment. Aha! Through creating, I was gaining access. So, what makes me think I am a revolutionary?

Revolution has to do with something that changes - often, completely - the late Latin etymology says this word means to roll back or revolving. For me, when I woke up in my twenties, I rolled back the myths placed upon me and, as soon as I could, I began to invite others to consider the entrenched beliefs and dominant paradigms. I held my first radical circles in high school; they were called the Rage Club. And it hasn't stopped since. Now I call them, 'Red Thread Circles'. Just ask my Mom.

I became interested in how the brain works, how it works with the heart and how we could find the missing

4

information in order to access and collaborate with our thought process. Have you ever had the thought: 'There has to be something more than this?' Well, that was my driving force - looking for more than a status quo worldview. If we can get access to that - won't we be able to inhabit our bodies and minds and make the differences we want to make in the world? I am counting on it. I quit my corporate jobs, turned down big book deals more than once, and even left art school to pursue this in community: How do we get in here to discover who we really are?

Who looks out with my eyes?
What is the soul? I cannot stop asking.
If I could taste one sip of an answer,
I could break out of this prison for drunks.
I didn't come here of my own accord,
and I can't leave that way.
Whoever brought me here will have to take me home.
~Rumi~

Well, who are we? We are creations (our bodies and souls), living within a creation (earth and cosmos). Who create all the time (our lives, communities and families). So, we must be truly conscious about what it is we are creating (our experience of life now and in the future).

5

We also must, as important as any other thing we do, allow our connection to our creative life force to guide us (our creative process). Otherwise, we will soon exhaust ourselves with our version of saving the world.

Our desire to serve can be woven with a tender understanding of ourselves as creations which create in order to thrive. Through intentional creating we renew ourselves, create patterns of resiliency, and can contribute to Creation as a whole. To become anchored with the certainty of what must be done, during uncertain times, starts with a powerful connection to our own soul work. For a conscious awake human, any other starting place will have us arrive at a destination other than the one that is most essential for us, personally, and therefore collectively.

The narrative about - 'What it is I have to say or not say' - has been running alongside my usual narrative of: "Create, no matter what." I am sure I am not alone as we ask ourselves what we can do - with our current view of world events. Clearly each voice does matter, and from a quantum perspective - it matters tons at the level of the tipping point.

We may be going uphill, but some of us have learned to run up hill, even with our dresses on fire. We were made for this.

Our desire to serve can be woven with a tender understanding of ourselves as creations that create, in order to thrive and be awake. Through intentional creating we renew ourselves, expand our imaginations, come up with brilliant ideas, and can contribute to Creation as a whole.

People operating in the collective without an awareness of self are dangerous.

What is the most the most essential thing right now?
I think the most essential thing right now is to ask ourselves each day - what is most essential for me today? What do I need to thrive instead of just survive? What meets my own needs, as well as makes a contribution to where I feel called?

My experience is that awake humans naturally CARE and want to serve the common good. Especially if that care is sparked by something that person LOVES and feels inspired by. When humans are asleep or numbed out (about things like water protection, human protection and rights) - we do not act in tandem for the highest good, but make choices in isolation.

The creative process is a saving grace not just for those who identify as creatives, but for all beings, because of how it impacts our body, our brain and our narrative of what is happening. When we create, we gain access to a collaboration with our deepest selves. We exit the self-imposed exile of disconnection to soul self. That self has information for navigating the future that rivals any other narrative. The only narrative that will work for you, is the one you create. All other narratives are over-rated and most often tainted with the fear. Fear and illusion are smoke screens put in place by the over-culture to keep us oppressed by systems not even designed for human beings.

This unfolding creation story, has need of you, showing up as vitally and uniquely you, and from this place, we will work together to embody transformation and act for change. The magic of your particular alchemy is what is the most essential thing. This is where the unique solutions will arise through collective imagination. Enclosed in these pages, although not obvious perhaps is my response to the US Paris Agreement, the US Election, the shootings in schools and churches and so much more.

Dear Reader, I must tell you, the order of poems is random. I longed for order or theme or chronological placement, but no. My Muse insisted I not make everything tidy and let it fall off the shelf for you at just the right time. Plus typos are included per usual. Open, point, read is one method. I contemplated calling these Prose Poems since they are not tidy little packages that are worthy of a word as hallowed as poetry. Yet it is the 'feeling' that this kind of writing gives me that makes words become medicine. And so poetry for me is a state of being, of awareness and certainly, prayer.

The childhood picture on the back cover is me playing 'house' in a closet with my toys at about 5 years old. I saw it as a kind of shelter and it seemed just right.

Shelter of the Sacred invites you to ponder your own creative urge and process. Because each of us gets to choose if we will be one of the ones who tends the sacred. I say yes as I invite you to join me.co

Signed on the last new moon of 2017
Santa Fe, New Mexico with scar-dust,

shiloh sophia

clouds, ashes, threads & roses : a dedication

For My husband, Jonathan McCloud. Who in solidarity changed his name to match mine. Poetry in motion and devotion. Who was present for the writing of all of this over the past two years. Who was not just present but also provoked, inspired, understood, and let me read them to him. Who made me coffee in the perfect recipe. Who is both healer, and guide. Who is a fine poet who has encouraged my own poetry through his own. Thank you for sharing the clouds of every sky with me.

For Terra Sophia, the mountain of my teacher. For the space you have held and hold. For many misty mornings since childhood, the smell of wood fire, eggs and collards we harvested from the coast on the stove. For being the place that holds the ashes of my teacher, Sue Hoya Sellars. This land, for reminding me what is important and providing a reference point for choice. Please continue to teach me the ways you have for me and how to tend you for your future. Thank you for being home in Anderson Valley, California.

To the members of the Red Thread community.
My tribe of irreverent and reverent Cosmic Cowgirls that light the cosmos with inquiry, comedy and perspective.

For Intentional Creativity Teachers and Guild Members. Women who get the work, carry the medicine and trusted me enough to work through the Talisman! Thank you for holding the torch for Intentional Creativity with me, for me, for those we serve, our Beloveds.

The Red Madonna Sisterhood. For being the shelter for the sacred heart of women and allowing Lady Church to find many forms in beauty.

Without each of you these wouldn't even exist, since I wrote them, for you. Thank you for being in all senses of the word, my inspiration.

For the women whose stories I have read these past two years to start many of my days from around the world. For what you have endured and live to tell. For those who have no voice, I offer roses at your altar. Roses tumbled from the dress of the Great Mother. Thank you to Lois Hermon of the Women's United Nations Report for the stories, who believed in me way back, and said, "One day, you will stand with me at the United Nations". For five years I came and held my red thread on that sacred, troubled ground. You showed me how.

For Mother Mary, my teacher and guide. Who showed up for me in my twenties and has never left my side. Thank you. With tear stained fingertips, I bow. Thank you for all the images, and the prosperity that you have brought through your image for me, and for those I serve in your name. For your son, Yeshua, who is everywhere I look for him.

For Musea Sophia, the future, the legacy, the idea of a dream so big I have to run to keep up with it. And yet as I run, I laugh. And as I laugh others join into the laughter. We are not racing, rather, we are dancing quickly into spaces we define ourselves for the creation of art, culture, justice and story.

For this good, green golden earth upon which I have my being. I am so grateful to call you home and to find myself here at this time. May I continue to learn from the wisdom, which is yours.

invitation

As you enter the poetry on the next page, pause...
close your outward eyes and open the ones inside.
It is with the inner eye that these story poem prayer rants
will have the most capacity to be wrestled with and savored
and put to use for good.

Perhaps a cup of tea is called for. The lighting of a candle.
The covering of a fuzzy blanket or woven shawl may add
comfort.

To choose to enter the shelter of the sacred is a conscious choice.
Something discovered on pausing and pondering.

Welcome.

we are the shelter of the sacred

No one is coming to save us from ourselves
We are the ones doing the saving
We cannot save ourselves by sleeping
We cannot save each other by angering
We cannot save the earth through complaining
Saving begins in the innermost temple
In the hidden places many of us have neglected.

Oh, my precious friends!
We are remembering now, aren't we?
Don't you feel that flow of life,
that fire of the spirit moving in fierce tenderness?
Regardless of what they say about the end of things,
we know we are ever and always the beginning.
We really do have the support we need for what's next
Let's enter into collaboration with that support
The coherent message of divine order is ever-present.

We know what to do
We must remember our assignment:
We are the shelter of the sacred
When it all feels like too much,
Tend the temple within and let that move out from you
See it reaching the others, still sleeping

See our communities waking and gathering

We have never been here before

Yet many of us walk here together,

Along the edges of the uncharted map of the future.

When we find each other, we can celebrate:

There you are! I have missed you!

To tend your own garden isn't some 'good idea'

This tending is essential

so that we might move mountains

Remember who you are

Remember why you came

Many of us, now, remembering and showing up

May the Creator of All reveal us to ourselves

May we dance in between each impossible space.

Our bodies and hearts and minds leaping ahead

Keeping time with the soul~birds in the cosmos

Come my friends, it is time to gather ourselves together!

The Council of the Sacred is upon us,

in each home, in each building, in each heart,

in each garden, in each land, in each hand,

in each conversation, in each agreement,

in each moment - we are calling this Circle!

prayer to the holy mothers

Illuminate for us
what we do not see
Resonate through us
what we do not hear
Reveal to us the sweetness
that we do not taste
Raise up within us
the places we have gone dead
Remind us of who we are
when we have lost the path
Nurture the empty bowl
within us that is hungry
Turn toward us
in the places we have turned away
Teach us
what we have not learned
Guide us
in the ways of wisdom
Teach us forgiveness
when we can't find it for ourselves
Weave for us
that which we have unraveled
Amen *12-12-17 Feast of the Virgin de Guadalupe*

17

will you be the one?

Will you be the one
to call us into circle?
To start the soup from scratch?
Will you be the one
that we can turn to
when the dark night is long?
Will you be the one
that remembers who you are
and reminds the rest of us.
Not with fury or condemnation
but invitation and even a bit
of unexpected romance.
Will you be the one
to invite us to a new myth
and show us how to begin
a sentence without scars?
Will you be the one
to say to the other ones, come!
Will you be the one to pray
To the Lady who untangles the knots?
Will you be the first to dance?
Will you invite me?

the Torchbearers show us how to make fire

The women who have kept the sacred flame lit
throughout the centuries are our ancestors

We will never know them by name
But they call us by our secret names

About them, we only know this:
They prayed for us to remember

"Remember that we must all
tend the sacred flame"

And if we don't, if we go to sleep,
women will come to wake us

We will hear the rumbles of their feet
stirring sleeping dust from our souls

We will feel the numbness part ~
wiping tired veils of unknowing from our eyes

You will hear them call you by name
You will not be able to resist any longer
"Remember…

You are made of stars
You are made for this life, this time, right now
You are the torchbearers of the future
No one can take your fire from you
It is time to light your torches"

When they dance, their hips, feet, bellies and
breasts create the friction of the ancients

Rubbing sticks together to make fire
they come rumbling into our consciousness

Little embers in our hearts
begin to send sparks, pow, pow, pow

Then we can see each other
and remind each other:

"There you are! Somehow, I remember you
Somehow, I have missed you, and this…
Let us go and wake the others
It is time to dance out of this long sleep"

This is how to make sacred fire:
Pass it from heart to heart

do what you desire

Do what you desire
not because you might die,
but because you might live.
The framework
from which you view your life
is informing all of your choices.
What do you choose?
What is truly essential today?
What does your heart speak?
Let's practice awakeness
and in that find presence
and in that, truly live.

something is happening!

I stopped waiting for something to happen!
I became the happening.
I no longer require evidence of love.
I am the evidence of love!
I am what Love looks like, right now.
I have long tired of waiting to believe.
No longer requiring the "showing up"
of the Blessed One.

I am the messenger of that
One who shows up!
I shall now study how the universe works
as my devotion.
Tree, stone, water, light, flower, star
are the infinite love notes!
Signs are scattered like seeds in a prism of love.
I am the witness.
Maybe the universe is waiting for us to notice,
to show us something.
Maybe we have been looking for love
in all the wrong places.
The perfect equation of creation
will be my lover now.

While we wait to prove God wrong
and lose our faith:
People will die. Nations will fall. Ideas will change.
Meanwhile: Miracles are born. Heroes rise.
Ideas change.

It isn't that I no longer see suffering.
It is that I see suffering without turning away.
It is that which is mine to do, that I must become.
This doesn't mean all our prayers
will get answered, they won't.
This doesn't mean healing will happen.
Sometimes it won't. Or it will.
If we require getting what we want
as evidence of God, let's give up now.

I have a new belief
that has taken root in my rainbow soil.
Every living thing has resurrection renewal particles
and waves, waving back at us.
When we dance with that mystery,
poison can give way to physics.

Quantum physics is the mother tongue of the universe.
While we are so busy trying to blow it all up

and parse it all to bits,
We are missing the point entirely
about how this works
and can work for us.

The stardust matriarch told me:
"Everything is made of stars.
We are cooling sacks of star dust.
This body is our cosmic address."
This isn't some concept perpetuated
by positive thinkers by-passing reality.

This is the happening we are happening in.
We are the alchemists.
We occur inside of a context
in which we are at cause to create.
One of the real questions is this:
What is your part in the great unfolding?

Can we begin to live as if our voice
and presence truly matters?
Then we enter the zone of 'Being the Happening'.
Instead of waiting for something to happen, like I was.
What shows up in your field is different
than what you saw before:

New worlds are revealed

because of how you are listening, seeing, being!

What if we could live like that,

awake and curiously on the great adventure?

I wish I could tell everyone about this happening.

This hallelujah happening,

that is happening all the time!

Survival is for cycles.

This kind of loving is for those who do the living.

We may not save ourselves,

or save what is sacred to us.

In the act of showing up

for our part of the red thread:

We become the happening

and invite other to happen too!

There are lots of us over here

having tea in the in-betweens.

Between the madness and the mystery

there is a glorious red thread café!

When you show up here,

we will remind you of who you are.

Don't wait to feel better

or to get the awaited good news.

What if your heart is ready
to throw open the doors!?

Here inside the happening,
I will meet you....
Together we will
discuss the mysteries of the universe.

We will weave our red, purple, scarlet threads
into something lovely to wear and to share.
This fabric of loving will
keep our knees and feet warm
while we spin tales by the star maps.

Day is breaking
and I have to go start the tea, darling one.
I have waited for you since forever,
and I am so glad you are here!

Something is happening,
and I don't want to miss it.

for those who desire to serve the divine

Have you been taught that the way to go
is to ask and ask for what you want?
Are you worn out with wanting?
Over and over and over we ask.

We ask until we are empty with wanting.
We 'learn' we are not filled
by voices outside the soul.
Yet we also 'learn' it is not good to be empty.
Taunting of the promises
we have yet to acquire.

To be empty and full at the same time
is the riddle of saints and sages.

Can you want what you have?
I ask myself this question almost as much
as I used to ask for what I want.

Sometimes it happens the way you want.
Often not.
Yet this method continues as if it is gold.
Maybe it isn't, or at least not in the way

we have been 'using' it.
Maybe it is using us instead.

Maybe continuing to ask
and falling short over and over
is causing a deeper discontent.
Have you thought of the price of not ever
having just want you want
because you have named it so many times,
you are clear on everything that it isn't?
What if you are asking a question
you have worn out?

I wonder if enough praise is returned
on desires that are granted.
Do you even know,
when you get what you want?
Do you pause and praise the One?
Do a happy dance, tell the world
or are you onto the next bigger thing?

What happens when the prayers go unanswered?
Do you turn? Do you turn in, turn away?
Turn on ourselves and find ourselves not worthy,
or somehow not asking

with just the right tone of voice?

Our mojo must have gotten mixed up

in transmission or translation, right?

(Why isn't this working for ME?)

Are we then undeserving?

Oh please,

let us wake from this slumber of self-condemnation

for not being able to create the reality

we think we want.

What we DO create, is our own experience.

Methods of asking are being hawked

by the bunches.

I myself, have tried many.

We wear out the night with incantations

of what we have been taught we want.

Will we pause and tune in to

what the soul requests of us?

What we might be made for or from?

When we lose it all again,

we will make stories up about all of it

that aren't true
in an effort to make sense of something
we were never intended to name.

Do you still think good people get good things
and bad people should then get bad things?
That is an idea from childhood long gone.
Then if good people don't get good things
they are doing something wrong?
Do you think this, about yourself
and your loved ones?

Set yourself free from this.

Consider this:
Instead of asking for what you want,

Ask:
What is wanted from me?

Then don't fill in the blank.
Wait on the Divine presence.
Wait and listen with the ears
you can barely hear.
I don't mean sacrifice

I don't even mean selfless service
I don't mean over-giving
and doing what is not yours to do
just so it can get done
and no one is as good at it as you are.
The reason to ask what is wanted from you,
instead of what you want is this:
You get a different answer for a long time.
That different answer reveals hidden things to you
that you would not see otherwise.
There, just there, in the in-between,
the holy place shines with loving!

Eventually, some fine day when you
barely expect it and have forgotten this practice
what you want and what is wanted
of you, come together.
Your supple invitation culminates
into coherent beauty.
Whooooooosh. This feeling is luminous!
A falling love that alchemizes
your antiquated mythos.

Consecrate the days you have with loving.
That is where the real receiving lives.

I know, we often feel desperate.

I have felt this too.

In times of desperation

I still resort to begging,

yanking on the universe

with wailing and rose petals.

But when I don't need to, I don't.

This teaching does not come easy,

practice is required.

Knowing when and how to ask

IS part of the equation,

yet it may be different than you have been taught.

If you have been asking for what you want

for as long as you can remember,

Try this:

Ask what is wanted of you....

And then see what happens.

You might be surprised.

And surprising yourself is a wonderful thing!

In this way, you become the offering.

Being the offering opens

so much more of you

to the mystery that was available

all around you

that you could not receive,

because all the wanting

was deafening the radiance.

You have become the talisman,

consecrated for loving.

May our requests become sweet prayers

in the presence of the Divine One.

we have been waiting for you

Let me be the one to tell you:
You are beautiful,
You matter to me,
You are wanted by all of us.
Your gifts are truly needed,
We have been waiting for you,
Yes! Specifically you.

The rest of us here on earth
are working out our stuff
right alongside of you,
remembering who we are too.
This is sacred work and
not everyone gets to do it,
because not everyone knows
this work even exists.
But you do.
since you are reading this.

Part of our remembering is
to un-mix the messages.
You know the ones:
Be unique, yet not too unique.
Yes, you are special.

34

Yet don't be too special
look good but not too good
Be smart but don't let the
others know just how smart.

Enough of all those!
Let's move beyond them
into integration.
as the best message is
just to be you.
You already know this.
I know it isn't easy.

That's why I am writing.
If you are you, then you
can bring out your
Great Work. You can't bring
out a great work being
someone else, for any reason.
Got that? Good.

We have anticipated your arrival
and in that anticipation
we have prepared a space for you
to happen in.
A space surrounded by loving.

Go ahead and be special,

Take up space,

Explore your unique-ness.

We aren't worried about

you getting a big head.

We need more people

with big ideas and the courage

to put them in place.

We are here to help with that.

If more people felt they really

had something to contribute

that was theirs to bring

to the rest of us,

we might be in a very different place

in our sweet old world.

Don't confuse being special

with ego, those two get lumped together

too often and it isn't necessary.

Some of us have created entire

systems to help others

remember their value.

For until you act from your value,

your gifts won't likely come into form.

Be interested in you and your imagination

and what wants to come forth from you....
Be as curious as you can possibly be.

I wish this could be more lovely
and poetic so as to lure you in with
the beauty of the writing. Instead,
I choose plain words to call you in
with the beauty that really matters
right now, which is your own.

Let us be the ones to tell you
we have been waiting for you,
Welcome, welcome, welcome.
The place you have always sought
is indeed, within you, yet
we are here to remind you:
Dive in! It's worth the risk.
You are worth everything
it takes coming home to yourself.

unloyalty to the soul

A soft green leaf
falls into your lap
and you cry and
you don't know why.

The tender veins
on the underside of the leaf
show you a vision:
The murky edge of a relationship
gone awry and suddenly you know:
You have been untrue,
to the primary relationship:
You.
You didn't know:
Now you do.

Patterns and beliefs
so entrenched they seem true.
We just don't know
where to look at first.
Our relationship to truth
has always been complicated.

The investigation into the residual
compost of unloyalty to the soul
finally becomes too much.
A muffled scream
begging to be heard
tears through our unrest.
This disturbance is
often necessary.

So restless, not sure why:
Perhaps you are getting closer…

Though we may have no
language for this anguish,
the scent of freedom opens
a crack in the dark wood of awareness,
dense with other people's ideas
Hey, how did those get in here?

A bit of us begins to awaken from
slumber and is astonished:
Truth is nowhere to be found.

Waking up means a re-evaluation
of all we held dear
Each relationship reviewed

with the tenderness of an
archeologist searching
for something valuable.
Go slow. Go outdoors.
Be in a space where
leaves of awakening
fall into your lap.

If you discover something
new and lovely
come to tell the rest of us.
Those of us searching
for new truths
will be having tea
in the great mystery.

how to tend the sacred flame

Don't be habitual,
Be unreasonable about changing your patterns.
Don't hide your light,
Together we illuminate the dark places on the path.

Don't keep telling the old wound stories,
Cause something new to unfold in your life today.
Don't keep looking for how you can be right
Seek instead, something much more interesting!

Ask yourself: How is who I am being,
keeping those I love, framed and trapped?
Ask Yourself: How are my beliefs
keeping my wings clipped and my mind small?

Ask Yourself: What is wanted and needed
in the world that also brings me vitality?
Ask Yourself: What am I still hiding, that my soul
is ready to reveal, because of how I am listening?!

Consider what would happen
if you truly lived from trust?
Consider that if you require proof
to trust the Divine unfolding, it won't.

Consider there is a way to trust
that hasn't occurred to you yet.
Consider turning all of this,
over to the Divine!

You could get on your knees
and give thanks for what you have.
You could raise up your arms in devotion
and invite a cosmic conversation.

You could choose to tend your sacred flame
simply by stepping onto your sacred path.
You could open your heart like a cathedral
and illuminate the universe with your presence!

Don't require evidence of love.
Be evidence of love.
Don't require things to go your way -
travel in the dark.

Don't stop when there is a rock in your path -
ask your creative fire to light the way though.
Don't block the love coming your way -
open all your doors with foolish abandon!

Allow grace, which is freely given,
to come into your innermost chambers.
Allow curiosity, as a state of wonder
to let you see with new eyes.

Allow the Blessed One to be your Beloved
because even when you think you are lost, you aren't
Allow your body to be the temple of the Holy Spirit
and tongues of fire will adorn your head!

May you find companions who recognize you
as one of their own.
May you tend the sacred flame of your companions
and you will find peace that passes understanding.

May you choose the quest of becoming,
instead of the illusion of having it all.
May you receive the messages the Divine is sending
through all of your newly opened doors.

mother mary ☀ a dream

Dearest Mama,

Flying into your arms today,
I remember.
I remember how I felt
residing within
the protection of your mantle.
Like I used to long ago.

Now it is gone but the memory
of it resides in my tummy,
thousands of white butterfly wings
winging through empty spaces.

Last night, I dreamed
I was singing the song.
The first song I ever wrote to you.
I was 22 then
and I had only just met you.
I woke singing it
from the dream world,
into this world,
the song was carried -

"Mother Mary, Mother Mary, Mother Mary
Hear our call. Hear our call.
We have forgotten who you are.
Forgotten who you are.
You are our mother, you are our mother.
Yes, you are.
We have forgotten who we are
Forgotten who we are,
We are your children, we are your children.
Yes, we are."

I wrote that song while driving
in my red pick- up truck
on a three hour drive
from Terra Sophia to San Francisco.
It was the most powerful song
ever to come through.

I thought of you then, as dark
as the cosmos, wrapped in a
red garment that held your stars
in place, light shining through
the weave of red threads.
Back then there was
no search function on the web:

black madonna, red mantle,

looking for my mother, goddess of this century…

I found you anyway.

I searched for you

in the red earth

and the greening of trees.

I searched for you in the tea by the fire

with my teacher the star-walker

where we talked of ancient women.

I found you in conversations with my mother,

about your son and your task

in giving birth to the light.

I searched for you through the fear,

that loving you

was somehow not acceptable,

that I would get in trouble

for bringing you to the front of faith.

Not less or more,

but everything now – from your matrix.

You became the context

in which my faith happened.

You still are. Without you, none

of this story would have happened.

(If only more of us could see this)

I searched for you
at the end of my paintbrush,
and I found you there!
You were waiting for me since forever.
Patient. Anticipating. Waiting.
I didn't know then, what I know now.
How women I would share
your image with, that they too –
would find you
at the end of their paintbrush
filled with prayers.

You knew. You told me,
I would give away
all that you gave to me.
I didn't understand.
I do now.

Intentional Creativity.
Tears now. Flowing. Freely.
~~~
The sweetness of this
waking with you
I choose you again today.
I know what that means.

Curled with my lover in a forest of trees
I rise up to write you this letter.

I never un-chose you.
I just somehow moved further away
from the original way that I loved you.
Which I miss so much.
Was it youth, innocence, desperation?
That made the connection so intense?
You were everywhere then.
Everywhere I was, you were.
Everywhere I am, you are.
I don't really know how to pray
in the way I would like to.
I am a communicant.
I am coming back
to the closeness, as much as I can.
When I don't feel it as a feeling,
I will lean into it as a knowing.
As a memory of an embrace
that never leaves me.
I will lean into devotion.
Show me the way.

She is bright and unfading.

She readily appears to those who love her.

She is found by those who keep seeking after her. She makes herself known even in advance to those who desire her with all their hearts. Someone who awakens before dawn to look for her will find her already sitting at the door. Taking wisdom to heart is the way to bring your thinking to maturity. The one who can't sleep at night because they are consumed with thinking about her will soon be free from worry. She herself goes about looking for those who are worthy of her. She graciously makes herself known to them on their path. She comes to them in each of the ideas that they think.

~Wisdom 6:12-16~

When I find myself in times of trouble

Mother Mary comes to me

Speaking words of wisdom, let it be

And in my hour of darkness

She is standing right in front of me

Speaking words of wisdom, let it be

Let it be, let it be, let it be, let it be

Whisper words of wisdom, let it be

~ John Lennon ~

cathedral of the heart

Let us dwell within
the Cathedral of Her Heart.
Let us keep choosing to be love,
no matter what.
Let us see what is called forth
from our deepest longings.
Let us listen to the messages
rising up from the resilient soul.
Let us rest into beauty
so that we may be encouraged.
Let us tend this sacred planet
as if we are her children.
Let us honor one another
so that we may learn how this goes.
Let us be strong enough to stand
for what we believe.
Let us allow our full colors
to be expressed in our lives.

The Together kind of leadership

Leading isn't something that happens alone.
It isn't a solo adventure into being brave
or being the best at all there is.
It isn't about hiding all your flaws
or making yourself look better than you are.
Lots of systems are set up that way
and we all know they don't work.
Leading is a together activity.
It is something we take turns doing
or we get too tired
and give up before our time.
Don't buy some bill of goods
about how good you are supposed to be
in order to share your gifts.
It isn't true. Just lead you.
And in that self-discovery
you will encounter those who
are also leading themselves.
These are the kind of people
to make friends with.
To have tea with. To dispel myths with.
This is the kind of leadership that
will guide the future:
The Together Kind of Leadership.

on speaking to those who live from the soul

On speaking to those
who live from the soul
during times of great change.

Do not tell me to move on.
Do not tell me to speak out
when I wish for silence.
Do not tell me there is a reason
for everything, I know better.
Do not tell me not to succumb to fear
when there are clearly things to fear.

Here is a way
to speak to those
who live from the soul
during times of great change.

Remind me it is good
to just feel how I really feel.
Remind me that I don't have to move on
before my heart is ready
or speak before I have found my words
to name this strange happening for myself.

We have exactly zero proof
that everything happens for a reason,
so don't tell me that either.

Sit with me in my fear
instead of asking me to move into love.
Especially before I have identified the dangers
around us, so I can remind us
of what to watch for
during times of great change.

Remind me it is good to just
feel how I really feel because this feeling
informs appropriate action in personal timing.
We all have personal timing and in navigating
these times, we must honor the individual timing
as well as the collective happenings.
I am allowed to make distinctions between me,
and the world unfolding around me. I have to.
Through this kind of presence,
which could banish our mutual exile
perhaps we can find time
for some tea and epiphany.
I will meet you there.

rainmaker : i should have known then

My Love,
The night you walked into my world,
you changed it forever.

I should have known then
when from your backpack,
as a magician, you revealed
two apples and two beeswax candles
and a good bottle of red wine.

My head went back.
My eyes narrowed to try to see you better
and I wasn't sure whether to be
delighted or suspicious or both.
Turns out both was appropriate.
As you do continue to amaze
as well as astonish and stir curiosity.
Some days I wonder how you could
be a dairy farm boy from West Virginia
and at the same time make me wonder
for the first few years if you work for the CIA.
You are just fascinating like that.
Knowing answers to unknowable things.
Whether that is your way through the Paris subway,

or the kind of caviar on a little Sunday blini,
or the brand of chandelier bobbles in a
Russian champagne bar in New York.

Did I say New York? What about the time,
the first time at the United Nations when
the tech guy never showed and you were
able to broadcast films for five women with
five different technologies on the fly.
Hum. Hmm. Ho. Hallelujah for someone
truly interesting!

How you are able to be so multi-dimensional
and yet so country boy-down-home in
the same moment is part of your intrigue.
You taught me enough quantum physics
to be dangerous and that is a good thing..
We fancy ourselves troublemakers.

You aren't from around here are you?
Hang out in this solar system often?
What'll you have?
"The Last Word," you say in the Peacock Alley
of the Waldorf Astoria while lounging on velvet.
listening to Leonard Cohen on the grand piano.
A vintage cocktail to go with the Pal Zaleri

tuxedo you brought when you moved in.

You had a borrowed suitcase, a pillow,

a tuxedo and a book of Rumi.

Yes, I should have known then.

Turns out that tuxedo came in handy

on one very special day.

That first night, that second night, one year

and 10 days apart. You said, "You knew."

Maybe I will never know what it is you knew

those two first nights, when on the seventh night

you asked me to marry you.

I. Just. Said. "Yes."

Why? You might wonder after only meeting

a man two times would I say yes to a lifetime?

Because you patted your shoulder,

indicated that was where my head went

and said something like, "This is your home now."

Girls are crazy about that kind of

country song eros

I call you Rainmaker.

Rainmaker and Husband.

Husband, today is your birthday and we are going

off an adventure but we start this day like

we do every morning for the past few years

waking up and saying,

"Good Morning, I love you."

With a cup of coffee, music, sleepy smiles

and poetry. Enough poetry to heal the world.

I will never find the words to say

What it has meant to me to have you in my life.

Whether that is learning how to smell

the envelope of a hand-blown glass

or explode in buttercream sandwich giggles or

listen to you sing the blues at a random open mic

or pet your hair for baby elephant hour

which only lasts a few minutes, but lasts all day.

Oh – and – how you look at me.

You see me in ways I don't see myself.

You have opened me to myself through pleasure

and possibility. And a good time.

I needed that. Needed the laughter and the loving.

Thank you for walking into my life

I should have known then.

And for that I give thanks to God.

For you, mysterious is an understatement.

This isn't our first rodeo

but this sure is the funnest one,

and the one I want to spend the rest of my life

riding into with you.

borrowed suitcase and tuxedo

Your borrowed suitcase

Held a tuxedo

Not just any tuxedo

One made just for your form

I wondered then

Who you might really be

The stories so large, so intricate

You are ever illusive, yet so very here

When you asked me to marry you

After three days home, I said, "Yes."

Let's be clear that by this time

We had spent less than four actual days together

We have been brave, my Love,

Brave in loving, in risking, in letting go

In going deeper and in finding new stories

At the center of the rose, we found home

Sometimes I feel like you don't know

Who you are because your genius is often hidden

By choice or by design or by unconscious, I know not.

Hence the reasons I seek you so fully

Forgive me my inquiries that never end

I find you fascinating and truly desire to know

If the key I have found to your heart grants access

To a blooming romance and friendship for ever

Forever might not be a place or time

But when one lover says it to another

We know what it means –

For as long as we can

I long to be in your arms

i want to feel everything

Are you blocking yourself from feeling?

Bracing yourself against sensual experiences?

Afraid of what will happen if you let it all in?

Are you afraid if you let the emotions flow,

they won't stop?

You aren't alone.

Let's create the context together

that it is safe to feel how we feel.

That blocking ourselves from feeling

is more dangerous

to our soul health than letting it all out.

At first we will be overwhelmed.

We may cry. We may become angry.

We may melt down. We may 'lose it'.

Sometimes we have to lose it, to find it.

We find ourselves after losing it.

I don't want to look away. I want to see you.

I want to love you as big and wide

as my heart allows

I don't want my fear of loving

and what might happen to stop me.

I want to feel everything.

our lady of supreme tenderness

We raise up our hands in praise and petition
Open up our hearts that we might hear
Divine guidance flowing through to us
and through us to others and Earth
We have lost our way as you can see
and it seems a miracle is in order
and we know you have access to those
Is it possible to return us to ourselves?
In such a way that we remember who we are
and what we were made for?
Allow us to feel the love that is most true
so that we can heal these wounds of fear
and join in true connection
We need this
Thank you for listening to our cries,
and for showing up all over the world
and especially in my heart today
May this prayer or ones like it be sent up
today to you from around the world so that
your love flows to all beings now

Amen

she will become stardust

Girl

She will forget the fairies for a while.

She will try to hide her skinned knees

behind longer dresses.

She will put down her crayons.

She will try to fit in, and begin to hide parts of herself.

She will stop singing to birds

and lose the bridge to her imagination.

She will wonder where babies come from.

She will, even at this age, think about having babies.

She will make friends with the underdog.

She will wonder who will love her.

She will pray to the sky.

She will remember just enough to find her way.

Teen

She will have circles with friends in the forest.

She will find a style that is her own and love it.

She will begin to doodle on her homework.

She will try to fit in, and then rebel.

She will sing in the band and in her car.

She will begin to bleed with the full moon.

She will, with support, try not to get pregnant.

She will join the march and fight for justice.

She will have her heart broken and break hearts too.

She will find God and pray to what she feels.

She will begin to wonder she has forgotten.

Adult

She will eventually remember the magic she holds.

She will take up her space, and it will take time.

She will recognize her crayons

have become paintbrushes.

She will stop trying to please everyone

and be relieved.

She will find her voice and speak it aloud

and be called irreverent.

She will begin to be asked

when she will have children.

She will then give birth to children or ideas or both.

She will call circles and call for revolution.

She will be loved and love like it is all there is.

She will rebel against religion

of any kind and yet follow a sacred path.

She will meet her Muse for the first time and heal.

Middle Woman

She will call the wise ones to gather in circle.

She will lose her style and find it again

and be called wild.
She will open a gallery to show off
her very large paintings.
She will be surrounded by people she loves
and that love her.
She will translate her gifts into teachings
that will serve many more than she imagined.
She will stop bleeding and howl at the moon.
She will be grateful for cycle of freedom
from obligation.
She will start a movement
that will last for hundreds of years.
She will fall in love more deeply
than she ever imagined possible.
She will choose again the life of Spirit,
on her own terms.
She will have tea with her Muse
at midnight and write poetry.

Elder
She will become a mystic who just knows things.
She will become an eccentric in leather and lace.
She will be recognized
for her many contributions to beauty.
She will bring her medicine basket

and people will heal.

She will write books by the beach and the mountains

with her many dreams.

She will build a red tent in her living room

for storytelling by candlelight.

She will be asked if she is a grandmother.

She will speak about the arc of injustice sees.

She will choose to become the lover of the universe.

She will talk with Spirit daily, she will pray to the earth.

She will become the Muse.

Stardust

She will become so thin she slips into another world.

She will drop her clothing and become the cosmos.

She will leave her images to be discovered after.

She will connect with the source beyond source.

She will bring her teachings with her where she goes.

She will have no bone, no blood,

yet she will be everywhere.

She will become the grandmother of the world.

She will inspire us to stand up

for what we want to save.

She will become love

and all who know her will feel that love.

She (has) will become one with her prayers.

She will become stardust.

this isn't a test.

This isn't a test.
There are no check boxes
that you missed.
No arbitrary line
that you have already crossed.
No way to fail this.
This isn't based on who is smarter
and who has more value.
This idea is a dangerous illusion.

This isn't a race.
There isn't a starting gate.
There isn't a finish line.
There isn't a prize for
going faster, better, longer.
There is nowhere to get to.
Exiting the race may
mean you enjoy this day
a whole lot more.

This isn't a game.
There are no other competitors
that you need to beat.
No made up rules by someone

who didn't have your best interest
at heart. No way to lose.
Even not showing up
doesn't mean you lose.
This isn't a game at all.

This isn't a dress rehearsal.
You don't need to spend your
time looking good and acting normal.
You don't need to look like
you are the best one for the position.
Just being who you are, isn't easy,
but it guarantees this isn't a dress
rehearsal that you can fail.
You already got the gig,
the one for which are perfect,
your own life.

This isn't a fight.
There is no one to beat up.
There is no referee calling
the shots. There is nothing
to win. That doesn't mean
there aren't causes to defend.
Don't enter the battlefield
with bravado and promises

of doom and dread.
It has never turned out well
for us in the end.

Start singing with your
whole heart about this.
There is no winner
if anyone loses. We know this.
The alternative is inherent
in releasing the
sword-wielding mentality.
Reclaim your consciousness
from the over-culture.
Today would not be too soon.

Stop trying to get ahead,
since it is costing you everything.
Is it time for a leap of faith
without an objective to get ahead?
Who would you be
without objectives and goals
to define your invented reality?
Maybe an even better idea
would arise. You never know.

Yes, we will die anyway.
Turns out that isn't the point.
We might end up living
instead of racing, pretending,
fighting. That sounds lovely,
doesn't it? Where is that
freedom…we know it exists?
We never stop looking,
yet it is closer than we thought.

Don't make a bucket list.
There is no list. There is loving
what you love and in that,
everything. What if we missed
the point? Is there a point?
We keep making up new
stories to justify the cruelty.
Yet as cruel as we are to
ourselves, we should start right here.
This isn't what we once thought.
Changing the contextual metaphors
may be one of the most important
decisions of our lives.

in times of great sorrow

In times of great sorrow,

may you learn to be with the knowing

and not lose your joy.

In times of great collective undoing,

may you maintain a strong connection

to your inner self.

In the journey of intense grief

may you feel everything

and not lose your way home.

In times when it seems the truth is lost

may you hold fast to what is dear.

When you are healed enough

may you reach out to offer blessings to others.

May the revolution we are in need of

begin to rise in the heart of our community circles.

And please, rest when you are tired.

We need you whole and ready to lead.

May this blessing go out to where it is needed.

Amen

secrets of the unicorn card

Those of us who secretly fear
we are a fraud
When outwardly we pretend to be cool
will find we are not alone in this...yet...
the persistence of pretending keeps us in line

For those who secretly fear
they are still buying into the system
Try though we might to resist,
we court anxiety with almond milk chai
We, who host a cement Buddha
from the drugstore on the doorstep
buy organic and go to yoga and
practice kindness, may find,
we are still asleep

For those who secretly fear
the energy of others will get on us,
will find we cannot preserve ourselves
from the messy containers of beings
We will discover these is no escape
from entanglement and finally-
stop trying to play the unicorn card
and escape this reality

For those who secretly believe
they are more special than everyone
must begin to realize that this secret
holds great responsibility
And while we need not surrender
to mediocrity or uniformity
May we be humbled until false veils fall
and reveal something fresh to behold

For those who secretly live in fear
yet must tend their family in love,
may you find the place where the
fear is no longer in charge
This is not to say there aren't things to be afraid of,
rather we shall not let the fear dominate
all of our experiences

For those who secretly hate their job
yet stay for money,
will find their soul will listen
if they just speak the truth
We will all have to do things
we do not wish to do
But maybe do it with awareness instead of denial

For those who secretly fear
getting sick with things like cancer
And fear that if they fear it,
they will bring into being
May you find freedom from the idea
that your thoughts will harm you
May your thoughts begin to create
in possibility your wholeness
while making room for healthy fear

For those who secretly fear their
ceaseless affirmations aren't working
All the fridge magnets and chants
you put in place to create
the reality you think you need and want
and have been taught to desire
May you create a true and sacred place practice,
Where you can hear your own voice

And in all this, may we find freedom
while honoring the secrets that stitch our
dreams together with lace,
leather and unicorn bone.

no need for hiding

For the women who secretly hold their abuse in silence
May the day come when the silence is no more
May the roar of justice be so loud
that all can hear and heal
Then there won't need to be a hiding place.
Can we believe?

For the men who secretly hold their shame in private
May the day come when you
can move beyond that imposed cage
The beauty of your being will be revealed in time
Then you can become who you secretly hoped you
always were
Then there won't need to be a hiding place.
Can we believe?

grieving america

Grieving America

If you do not speak for the earth

You do not speak for me.

If you do not care for the water

You do not care for me.

If you do not protect our skies

You do not protect me.

If you do not see our fiery sun

You do not see our food is on fire.

If you do not preserve our lands

You are destroying our home.

If you do not listen to the creatures

You do not listen to any of us.

If you will not put human life before greed

You do not speak for us.

In the wake of the Election

i don't want to impress you

I don't want to impress you.

I refuse to perform to make you love me.

Looking good is exhausting.

Especially if you have to keep it up.

Being right is so last life time.

I am not invested in hiding to protect myself.

This doesn't mean I am surrendering.

This means my soul has plans for me.

I just want to be as I am called to be.

I am spontaneous, a badass, unpredictable at best,

and if you still love me, awesome. I love you too.

I would much prefer to play together

than look good by myself.

I don't care about being right,

I would rather just be with you. Okay?

This doesn't mean I am surrendering.

This means my soul has plans for me.

You know this already-

to be yourself takes crazy courage.

The kind most of us are born with.

But somehow, we tuck it away to protect others.

Or, even worse, we forget.

People can be afraid of people like us,

and try to shut us down

It isn't too hard, since we don't want to offend.

That doesn't mean I am surrendering.

This means my soul has plans for me.

When we are too shiny, we scare people.

That's okay. Tell them what all the sparkle is about.

Tell them your shine has spilled out,

that the edges of your container have expanded.

Invite them to dance in the scattered radiance.

Tell them not to surrender to the way things are.

Tell them, their soul has plans for them.

she eats lightning for breakfast

This night,
She is shedding the skins no longer needed
Heavy trench coats shaken off on the dance floor
As she moves her body she feels the electricity build
A lightening up of all the heavy hearts held inside
Turning towards the shadows with wide eyes
She says, "I see you, shadow stories.
Thank you, for your teachings.
And… you are not my master."

This dawn,
She declares -
I will not hide from myself
I will not turn from suffering,
I will not let fear dominate my experience
I choose to eat lightning for breakfast!
I have lived through the sorrows needed
To shape the self that is mine to become
And I will love with an unreasonable appetite
For loving what is hard to love.

This day,
She dances weightless through the crowds of chaos
No longer fearing attack or needing protection

Finding a freedom that is chosen,

The kind that exists even in the middle of war

She finds the needs in the world,

Unique to her gifts

She nurtures them, unafraid, knowing,

Deeply knowing,

The Great- Spirit has chosen us

To do a great work

And each of us is preparing ourselves

For the journey ahead.

This time

Is not a time to be 'out there'

Without being 'in here.'

Each of us doing the work we need

To do to get free of the stories

That are keeping us from serving beauty

Dance with me through the chaos

Because I need you

As long as we are in our own way

We cannot go where we are most needed

This is the strange medicine, that in tending the

Wounds of the world,

your own wounds are tended

Your time,

This is your time simply because you are alive.

The mystery has brought you

A sacred assignment.

Your piece of the red thread is pulling you forward.

Listen up, you don't need to save the world.

You don't need to save yourself or get it right.

Lay down those heavy thoughts to discover

your time has arrived, just show up,

Because of you:

What can be saved, will be saved.

This is more than enough.

This is why she eats lightning for breakfast.

A great force of light comes through her.

She can block it or bear it

The heat is intense,

Sometimes it threatens to consume, annihilate

She turns the lightning into prayers.

ask for what you want

Ask for what you want.

You might not get it.

It might not be what is to be, for now.

Asking is not all about getting.

Rather, it is about feeling longing.

About allowing hope to rise up.

About feeling into the places that scare you.

When we let ourselves feel it, we set something free.

Captured birds suddenly fly from our hearts.

This is a great mystery.

So, when you ask, try not to dominate.

Try not to always be striving to achieve outcome.

With hands open, implore, pray, offer, seek.

Surrender your desire on the altar of possibility.

If you don't receive it, don't blame yourself.

Life is much more complex than that.

We don't always get what we think we want.

And sometimes we don't get what we need either.

Yet still, ask for what you want.

Then with a heart raised to the sky, watch.

Witness the unfolding of life.

Allow awe to be your framework.

Offer yourself to this potential. Show up.

Yes, show up for your want

but allow for the unexpected.

In the between spaces,

beauty will be revealed.

poor life choices

Poor life choices

make awesome legends.

Our future self

is forged in the fire of stories gone wrong

and failures we tried so hard to avoid.

Include everything within the context

of Mystic-Badass-in-Training.

Your Legend belongs only to you.

Don't confuse failure for sadness

and happiness for success.

There is so much more to life than that!

You got this!

Are you trapped in your patterns of belief?

In how you think things are? What if you are wrong?

What does transcending your ideas look like?

Out beyond ideas of wrongdoing and rightdoing,

there is a field. I'll meet you there.

When the soul lies down in that grass,

the world is too full to talk about. Ideas, language,

even the phrase "each other" doesn't make any sense.

~Rumi~

beyond cause and effect

Dear One,

Our ideas, traditions, and beliefs

are keeping us from accessing

a whole other world

Expanded Sensuality and Access to Genius

may be hiding behind limiting ideas:

light/dark, masculine/feminine.

Are you up for a deep dive into possibility?

Chances are you've had this conversation before.

I know I have.

But somehow I keep "forgetting"

and or going to sleep

on how to really LIVE INTO

this other way of experiencing

what could be possible

if I moved beyond ideas of cause and effect

as the only two potentials.

Let's look at this kind of thinking:

Either/Or

Masculine/Feminine

Light/Dark

Cause/Effect

Free/Caged

Success/Failure

Lack/Abundance

Right/Wrong

Healed/Sick

Fear/Love

Flow/Strive

All/Nothing

Win/Lose

Above/Below

Inside/Outside

Black/White

This/That

Doing it right/Not doing it at all

What I want to ask us is this:

What's over there in the in-between?

In the in-between spaces and places.

Life happens in the middle of them.

Or is there another place?

When an electron changes

what it is doing

because we witness it,

we only see it here or there.

There is a whole other 'thing'
it is doing, a whole other set of potential
behaviors that we don't get to see.

I'm after THAT.
What we are not seeing.
The space between the visible
and invisible is where I like to hang out.
World between worlds

What if....
It's not either/or
but something mysterious
and beautiful
between the two
that transcends
the titles and their
assigned meanings.
Is it a reductionist view
that may be limiting us?
Or something else?
What's the dynamic bridge between
For you? What arises?

Do you hear this a lot or say this to yourself?

I am not in the flow.

There is either fear or love.

We have to bring the light.

I don't want to fail.

I want to work in the feminine.

I don't want do things the masculine way.

Really, it is in many conversations.

Dare I say, most?

Listen for it now – personal descriptions

that are held in this paradigm.

Yours and theirs, ours.

If I was doing this right, I would be creating abundance.

This shouldn't have to be so hard, if I was in alignment there

would ease.

If I do this, then that will happen. And I don't want "that."

Assumptions. Invisible constraints. Cages.

Do we need them?

Can we learn to live more in there?

Even those of us who claim to be conscious

find ourselves within this limiting language.

How do we move along the continuum?

And what of beauty?
Beauty has everything to do
with allowing us to see what we are not seeing....

My love says these either/or is a divine dichotomy:
"They need the other state in order to be.
It makes no value judgement between
what's right and wrong, but the middle path.
Equilibrium, balance, harmony, not stasis".

When I first met my love, I would give him
two choices, this or that. He would almost
always say, YES.
In Newtonian physics for every
action there will be an equal and
opposite reaction.
Our "yes" moves us
beyond that previous model of
if this, then that. Is this true still,
yes. Is it not always true?– Yes.
'Cause and effect' are not always true.

There's more.
I don't have answers. I have questions
Getting this hidden thinking conscious is my hope...
Curiosity is my probe into consciousness.

89

We are told it is so. This either/or.
This is what we already know.
A fixed world.
Then there is what we don't know.

What if this was really about discovering
YOUR way –a way consistent with your being
and your story that you are causing?
Would access to your way of moving
move you beyond the light/dark,
the right/wrong? Would a whole
series of choices be revealed for you
that were hidden before?

Art, poetry, music, and creativity
reveal to the senses, the alchemical bridge
between worlds without cancelling
one thing or the other.
We see both places
and the way between.
The dynamic interplay
of pre-conceived polarities
is resolved if only for a moment.
Then it's gone again.

neither love or fear

One day I moved in neither love nor fear,
I found a new place.
I could have stopped at, "Don't be afraid," but
I realized I WAS afraid – and so there
was more truth to be had.
'Feel the fear and
do it anyway', as they say.

Someone recently asked me,
isn't it all about love?
Aren't you just guiding people
into love with your work?
I said – no – strangely enough.
I am not trying to get them anywhere
but to the next right place for them on
their path.

If I have a preconceived
idea that I am leading them to LOVE
even if I am operating in love,
Then…
I have laid a constraint on their experience
that I am defining for them.
I don't want to teach love or fear as a choice.

We are all at different places on the path.

A dear one may actually need to go into anger

or despair and the last thing I want to do

is make them feel like they need to go

into love in order to get where they are going.

This is how I love them.

I learned this spiritual perspective

from a transgender being

named Francis on her way to becoming

a woman in a red dress and high heels who was

In LOVE with Jesus. Married she said.

straddling

Cosmic Cowgirls

is the work of story and metaphor.

Inherent in the words Cosmic and Cowgirl

you have stars and earth.

A woman straddling the worlds.

We believe poor choices

can become great

legends to unfold,

IF we choose.

Only your imagination

can show you about how this works.

Your own myth reveals to you what

you can't see. Now that's cool.

By entering an imaginal world,

we find the hidden things that

have been waiting in the wings for

our attention.

Poor choices make great material.

your part

What is your part in the great unfolding?
Do you have a piece of the Red Thread
that is yours to hold? Ask yourself.

Are you a keeper of the sacredness of water?
Are you the tender of the flame?
Are you the one who turns the soil?
Are you the one who listens to the wind for wisdom?
Are you one who stands in both worlds
dancing in polarity?
Are you one of the star beings
navigating the cosmos?
Are you the one who loves us into waking?
Who are you and what is your part?

*The woman was given the two wings of a great eagle, so that
she might fly to the place prepared for her in the wilderness. ~
~ Revelation 12: 14 ~*

sbrogliare

English translation: Unravel. Disentangle.
Tease out. Clear. Unsnarl.

a. happy. birthday. pilgrimage.

watermelon pink polka dot linen dress
rendezvous at the Trevi Fountain
strawberry granita and church bells
prosecco on the rooftop with seagulls
fuzzy white robe – white sheet therapy
blue lit underground baths and steam
conversations with the Eternal City of Roma
cafe with Pope Francis at the Vatican
he speaks of love and Christos to all
standing with nuns in pale blue
drawn by the Black Madonna of Loretto
I didn't know where she lived but
she found me suddenly breathless at her feet
lighting candles for the Red Madonna
fresh bread with olive oil and salt
birds-eye view of everything
golden hoops from my lover
red lipstick kisses on shaded street corners
46 today. a grown-up woman today

I feel different today. complete. ready.

full moon rising over Rome.

questions on my lips:

where is the ample crossroads

between generosity and prosperity?

why does this age feel so different?

is there anything you want to show me,

my God?

buonjourno

June 19 ROME

the birds of St Francis of Assisi singing

whispered prayers into stone

tombs of saints and sinners

olive wood spoon for soup at home

Brother Sun, Sister Moon at midnight

Madre Bella Donna Maria gazing

ancient stories unfurling

lasagna made by Nonna fresh today

artist, Alberto, buying art, giving blessings

carrying alms for those who ask

magnifying glass reveals 4 chin whiskers

strega gelato – limone

sacred stones and monks moving quickly

Minerva temple now the Madonna temple

Roman columns remembering change

questions on my lips:

what would it mean to fully serve?

what would it look to live without fear?

what would St. Francesco think of all this?

did he really say?

S/He who works with his hands

and his head and his heart is an artist.

That is what I am.

buon pomeriggio

June 18 ASSISI

pecorino. pecorino. pecorino. Montalcino

tartuffo. Black truffle madness.

fatto a mano pici pasta every day

making love in the afternoon

sun on my skin, soft from swimming

Brunello and women-made wines

approaching a crossroads in myself

Not maiden, not mother, not crone or

medicine woman or queen?

sleeping in nesting nooks in swinging beds

thermea volcano water sacred bath

Catherine de Medici keeping me company

round white sunglasses and no shoes

opera in the lobby with ruffled pale pink shirts

Bagno Vignoni where Lorenzo the Magnificent bathed
visiting Catherine of Siena for insight
watercoloring endless magenta leaves
nothing to do
prayers for brothers and sisters
questions on my lips:
what's next? how do I live differently?
what is freedom?
Buonasera

June 17 TUSCANY

a red leather book bound in Firenze
hand-stamped in gold: Mothership
from my beautiful husband
signed with women's names
fingerprints of gold, witnesses. Accomplices
and one man
feasting with friends at Buco Mario
dreaming of uncoiling Diva x
13 original paintings of sbrogliare
who is the artist within the artist?
tiramisu and Illy café in tiny white cups
Minerva rooftop lounge chairs
the kindness of strangers
prayers spoken at every icon and altar

candles lit at Santa Maria Novella

the church floor marks summer solstice in gold

I am painting arches royal blue with gold stars

the ancient perfumery

pomegranate candles, queen's perfume

lavender soap, vitamin cures, rose liquors

Botticelli and I spend an evening

a week of art history and women, my style:

fall in love with the world to understand anything

the color aqua green walls with white roses

handmade Zecchi watercolors with honey & sap

lots of Fabriano paper, thick cream white

chianti for breakfast overlooking everything

street musicians come over to play for us

to light up our salon with Hallelujah

long evenings in small palaces

chandeliers and limoncello shots go nicely

smiles, so many smiles and happy faces

the study of ancient guilds and coats of arms

designing a logo for the future

I think we shall open a museum.

questions on my lips:

when can I come back?

why does Firenze feel like home?

what does Michelangelo have to show me?

how can I tell Artemesia thank you?

how do I serve you, with my gifts, Dear God?

a truly beautiful life

still I am thinking of you. as I do.

where you are. sending love.

mixing business and pleasure

colored banners flying from my buildings

reading: gratitude

a. happy. birthday. pilgrimage

art isn't just for artists

Art isn't just for artists.

It is for all of us.

It isn't just for those who are gifted

or show promise with skill.

Art is more like a soul language

that speaks to us from within,

if we are willing to listen.

For me it sounds like:

this day is a special day,

not like any other day.

you get to say things

feel things

and do things that

have never ever happened before.

that is very exciting.

don't imagine that you have seen it all.

for that is the only time your truth

will be hidden from view

until you wake up

to what's new, which is every moment.

which is now.

a new day to fall in love

and tell others you love them.

a new day to write

and find honey on your tongue.

to paint with a color and stroke

that you have never known.

being a true artist means

you are listening in your soul.

it doesn't mean

you make pretty things (but you might)

it doesn't mean

anyone says it is good (but they might)

but it does mean this:

listen with the inside ears

and see with the inside eyes.

Something, just here in the in between,

is making a path to your heart in this very moment.

if you listen, you won't be lost any more,

or alone.

Consider this:

Pick up a pen and paper.

Listen from the inside.

Write/Draw what comes out.

For in this way you change the future.

reckoning cave

My dreams did not come true.
My ideas of how this life goes crashed down.
I entered the reckoning cave
wearing garments of disillusionment
and bringing a journal and many black pens
to get it all down and write it all out.

It was a fine day when, finally
curiosity got the best of me.
A luminous mist entered the cave
and gently rolled the rock away.
I had done my time and I was ready.
'Every cave has its cycles,' I said to myself.

I claimed my time in the darkness
as my mourning for the old dream.
Then I put on the new dress
that curiosity brought along.
It was brightly colored, of course,
and stitched together with red threads
and purple ribbons, made just for me.

I found the nearest café and took out my journal.
"This is a new day," I wrote, somewhat cautiously.
Looking around to see if anyone
would challenge this idea
or tell me it was the same day as before.

Sipping my latte I had a brilliant idea arise!
Instead of choosing a new dream
I witnessed what my life had revealed
through the living of it.

I looked for new language for my experiences.
I decided, that although at times I didn't think
I could go on, I had survived, and I have stories to tell.

Perhaps others too had broken dreams
and needed permission slips to move along
to a new day waiting to happen.

broken dreams and doomed ideas

Dear Ones
of the Broken Dreams and Doomed Ideas,
This is a new day.
That it is a new day
doesn't mean everything
will begin to go your way or that new dreams
will magically appear.
However, I am here
to remind you that you are the one
who gets to choose that each day is a new day.
And for today, that could be good enough.

I don't think we need to be able to trust
the universe that good things will happen
because bad things will continue to happen.
I don't think we need to be able to trust
the Creator will answer all our prayers
because that lives in the great mystery.

I think perhaps instead of requiring life to conform
to our ideas, we try something altogether radical:
We choose to show up for our sacred assignment,
and we watch and we witness.

I don't know if it will work but I know dream domination has downsides and disillusionment. What if we asked - What wants to happen now?

recovery from cause

Have you been blaming yourself for being sick?
Blaming yourself for being injured? Tired?
Overwhelmed?
It is bad enough
when we feel this way anyway –
but to make matters worse
we also blame ourselves for it.
This isn't working.
blaming ourselves just isn't working.
Have you been blaming yourself
for being tired or overwhelmed?
And are you saying it is because
you work too hard?
Do too much?

I want to tell you something VERY important.
You can slow down
without needing to make yourself wrong.
You can practice self-care now,
without needing a reason.
Whether we work too hard or not,
we are feeling it.
All of us are feeling it,
for either ourselves or our loved ones.

Yes, I know it is a sign to slow down.

Go ahead and adjust your pace.

But consider instead not making yourself feel like…

somehow you deserve this.

We are driven, inspired, far-seeing visionaries.

We are doing sacred work no matter where we work.

We move because we feel called to move.

Because we can.

And sometimes because we have to.

I just wanted to tell you today,

If you are sick or injured:

You have permission to rest.

You don't need to blame yourself

or your body or faulty intuition or your company or job.

You can just, stop

and be in the being-ness of your body.

And listen for messages.

IF you listen without the filter of shame

clarity will arrive, instructions will come,

ideas for change will emerge.

You don't have to believe you caused everything.

You can if you want, if that is truly helpful for you.

I just want to ask you – is it helpful?

Often it is, to a point. To see where to adjust.

Even people who aren't working the way you are,

are having challenges, it isn't just you.

The world is changing.

Our ideas need to change with it.

The treatment of our earth, our water,

our food, our waste, our governments,

insurance policies, institutions,

are not consistent with creating well-being.

And so, it is not just us

who are creating this for ourselves.

We are all experiencing a need to protect,

the sacred and our sacred experience.

Including our right to health and well-being.

What we are really talking about here

is what you believe about CAUSE!

When you get into the finer print of the conversation

about whether things happen for a reason.

It is not a truth unless it is true all the time.

So, everything does not always happen for a reason

100% of the time.

This is about CAUSE

– Was it **caused** for a specific reason or outcome?

Or do we make it a teaching by choice? Or both?

Was there something behind the happening,

that made it happen?

Of course – no one knows,

but it might mean

everything doesn't happen for a reason.

Do we need it to – if so why?

This isn't about creating agreement –

this is about inviting a new conversation.

You are a powerful woman being.

You can adjust because it is time to adjust.

Not because you have done something wrong.

That is a paradigm of thinking that needs some

adjustment.

A recalibration is being called for.

You are a part of that.

A shame free space

that empowers you to make changes.

Because it is time.

Not because you are wrong.

Let your body speak all during your life,

not just when you aren't well or you are overworked.

Settle in for a cup of tea and a nap to recover from cause.

awake or asleep

An awake person is a conscious being,
open to what there is to see and be.
An asleep or unconscious person
is not open to seeing,
what they are not seeing, or being,
and may not be interested in doing so.
An awake person knows their own bulls**t
and can laugh about it and work on it.
An asleep person doesn't know their own bulls**t
but can laugh about it if they see it!

An awake person chooses to see something
larger than their self, like the great unfolding,
and participate in and contribute to it
as authentically as possible.
An asleep person doesn't believe
they have a necessary part in the great unfolding,
or that there is something called the great unfolding.

An awake person is generally aware
of becoming conscious,
and the time before they were awake
feels different for them – a pre-awake state,
there is a clear sense of before and after.

An asleep person may not know
there is something called awake and asleep.

Awake people seek to wake others up
so we can be conscious and curious together.
An asleep person is not seeking to wake others up,
and may often be attached to their state of
unconsciousness.
Just as attached as awake people are
to being awake.

To an awake person,
staying asleep doesn't feel
like an option anymore.
They become attached
and inspired by the possibility of further presence.
An asleep person may feel that
they don't have choices
and may not have considered
falling in love with everything as an option.

An awake person knows that to have
meaningful relationships, they have to discover
not only compassion for others,
but practice deep authentic listening.
Their need to justify themselves lessens over time.

An asleep person tends to be very 'me' focused,

selfish even, wanting their needs met above others,

can be lacking compassion, and justify themselves a lot.

An awake person may think they are awake,

and while they may be aware of others

who are asleep, will work towards

understanding and service,

instead of blaming the sleepers.

An asleep person may sometimes think

they are awake, and that others are asleep around them,

and easily move into blame.

An awake person is aware and inspired –

by being in awe and in love with the universe and others,

their own creativity, and they seek beauty.

An asleep person may not be aware

that they have the power to impact

their state of being,

or even how to approach doing so,

if they did know.

An awake person may try hard to be awake

and become defensive about the places

they are still asleep and not even know it.

An asleep person may find those

who are trying to be awake, quite humorous
and airy fairy or artsy fartsy or new age, elitest or, not
like them or even an as****e

Awake people look for other
awake people to hang out with
(to justify and validate their views)
Asleep people don't look for other
asleep people, they just find themselves with them.
They may however find themselves
drawn to awake people, and not know why.

An awake person generally wants to have
THIS CONVERSATION RIGHT HERE
about what those who are awaken
and those who are the sleepers.
And others like this...
about the nature of the universe,
the soul and the fabric of reality.
An asleep person may not know
this conversation is being had, or
that they could choose to be a part of it,
as a part of their waking up process.

Being awake is a choice, not a default setting,
and can be called upon by a sleeper.

Being asleep is the default setting,
and awake may not occur as an option,
let alone a desirable one.
Awake people can choose

happiness and goodness.
Asleep people can choose
happiness and goodness.
Awake people know that
the more they know, the less they know –
and that it is never ending and
there is always more to wake up to.
Asleep people also know there are
a lot of things they don't know,
but might not spend their lives seeking it out.

Awake people are called to change the world.
Asleep people can be woken up
to their capacity to change the world.
They know it needs to change,
they just don't know how important they are
to being a part of the change.
Awake people reading this will find
all kinds of things I got wrong and
will want to write their own.

This is the nature of awake beings. We see stuff.
And complain a lot about the sleepers.

Asleep people may wonder
if they are already awake and
what the fuss is all about anyway.

Awake people may see this entire inquiry as futile or,
perhaps have them consider
their own frame of reference, bias or opinion.
Asleep people will be sleeping
when this comes into their inbox.
One day may those asleep and those awake,
together, create a future worth living into.

"The world is violent and mercurial – it will have its way with you. We are saved only by love – love for each other and the love that we pour into the art we feel compelled to share: being a parent, being a writer, being a painter, being a friend. We live in a perpetually burning building and what we must save from it, all the time, is love". ~ Tennessee Williams ~

illuminated

May your mind be illuminated

May your heart be ready

May your spirit be delighted

May your body be your temple

May your hands be creative

May your feet find the path

May your ideas be inspired

May your prayers be heard

art is ritual

Creating art is ritual
when we choose for it to be.
In our work with Intentional Creativity
we bring mindfulness and beauty
to every aspect of our work.
From setting up the paint
to blessing the jar of water.
Things that were mundane
begin to light up as integral
to the journey.

All life is sacred
when we engage with it in this manner,
we come alive and beauty is saving!
Let's live like we are living
instead living like we are waiting
for something else to happen!

What if this is it?
And what if this is exactly
what will bring us to the next place on the path...

being yourself

being yourself
takes courage in world
where you are bullied
to be someone you aren't.
resist, and persist
in the expression of you
that calls to be revealed.
we need you as you are,
not as you wish to be
or as others say you could be,
but as you are.

love flow

Let's open our arms
raise up our hands
let the love pour in
let the love flow out.
This love is all around us
let the resistance fall away
and the fear dissolve.
Gratitude will light the path
in the uncertainty, we must shine on
reflecting the light to one another.
There are so many other things to do,
be, and say right now,
yet nothing may be as important
as this today.
Share your love.

*"We aren't running away from something.
We are running towards something" ~ Sue Sellars ~*

the constellation of you

We are creations
living within a creation
created by a Creator.

We are created to create.
When we create
with sacred intent
we align with the essence
of creation, as creators.

When we create
unconsciously without thought
for creation, we unweave
that which has been woven.

Our specific identity is an organization
of cosmic intent, particles of potential
in a design so impossibly beautiful,
if only we knew, who we really are.
Cooling sacks of stars
filled with the glory of Creator's
intention for us.
Stewards of creation, through our creativity.

The perfect conditions are supple
and the summoning of your particular
cellular enclosure is humming with causation.

What will you cause and create?
The origin story of the fire in your blood and bone,
remnants of expanding stars reaching earth.
Your cosmic address is the constellation of you.

You are created to create!

scar-dust

The missing never ends.
It deepens and carves
shaping the soul and story
in tenderness but made
from scar-dust.
Scars of loving worn outside.
I cannot hide this missing.

Last night I dreamed you came to me,
to my very house.
You opened the front door,
knowing how excited I would be to see you!
Like Jesus revealing himself
to Mary Magdalene, you too
looked like the gardener,
and surprised
me just as much.
Teacher!

I ran to you and fell into your arms.
I sobbed. We both knew the time
was short, the veils were thin,
and I wondered if you snuck out.
It was after all, Samhain.

I cried and cried in your lap,
I was sad, but you were not sad
in the same way I was.

I could see the soft folds of your skin,
the tender eyes of knowing.
Did I even smell your forest scent?

I told you everything.
Everything I already told you
and never got to tell you
with as much love
as I would have liked.
As you too, would have liked.

I told you about how
we have learned how
to honor you and your teacher
before you.

I told you what I am working on.
I told you about all the teachers.
I told you the language we have
claimed as our own.
You would be so proud, I said.

124

But you already know, don't you?
You wouldn't say.

I was looking for approval
For your yes in death
just was I was in life.

This scardust becomes stardust
only when I am not looking.

*For Sue Hoya Sellars, teacher, guardian, mother of my soul
and your teacher, Lenore Thomas Straus*

*Woman, why are you weeping?" Jesus asked her. "Who are
you looking for?" Thinking He was the gardener, she said,
"Sir, if you have carried Him off, tell me where you have put
Him, and I will get Him." Jesus said to her "Mary". She
turned and said to him Rabonni, which is to say, Teacher,
Great Master. ~John 20:16~*

a call to falling in love today....

Everything is alive to the noticing soul.

Falling in love with life

is not a default setting.

It is a conscious choice,

sometimes moment by moment.

To begin the free fall,

start with your sensual experience of

being human ~-

become mindful of the tastes, sounds, scents, feelings,

and knowings.

To do this you pause

and choose to be intimate with

the moment in a fresh way

as if you have never had that experience before....

Yes, the universe responds to this kind of attention.

We live in a witness/witness world -

how you interact with the clouds, the trees,

your loved ones, your own heart, the quality of the light,

the hours of the day, all changes how it responds to you.

We all know this, yet somehow we forget

and fall back asleep.

This quality of aliveness

gives the missing energy that is available.

There is a potential for more

beautiful experiences in every day, all day...

even in tandem with the suffering.

This day is made for rousing you from sleep....

Everything is alive to the soul

that notices what there is and

chooses how to relate with it.

We are all in relationships all the time - it is essential

to choose how we show up in those relationships.

Your presence, attention and sensual being-ness

can also wake others. We do this dance together.

We are the shelter of the sacred –

it is a practice

and it is the practice of a lifetime.

Let's practice and fall in love....

Tyranny of the Talented

Should the unschooled write? Dance? Paint? Speak?

Should anyone who doesn't know the rules

Attempt anything new?

Should we standardize self-expression markers?

Should we correct every mistake?

Because there IS a right and wrong?

Somehow we should all know what it is.

And if we don't know what is

accepted as right, we must find out.

Should we be quiet for fear of getting it wrong?

Of course, not.

And yet. We often limit the rogue voices.

Within ourselves and in others.

We filter them out.

We filter our wild muse for fear of what she/he will say.

We might not be able to take it back.

They might see who we are, after all.

"The ultimate tragedy is not the oppression
and cruelty by the bad people
but the silence over that by the good people
~Martin Luther King~

morning ritual

Do wake and pray

Don't turn on the devices

Do look outside at the colored light

Don't start to think about work

Do turn on the kettle

Don't get dressed right away

Do pick up a book of poetry

Don't complain to anyone nearby

Do stretch your body

Don't think about politics

Do give thanks for another day

Don't follow anyone else's advice

Do create a morning ritual

Don't resist gazing into your teacup

Do choose to be connected to life

Don't think twice about going to the canvas

Do revel in the time you have created

Don't wait

Do it today

you must have mistaken me for someplace else

You must have mistaken me for someplace else
I am not the countryside with rolling hills
log cabins and lazy days of rolling in the hay

I love the land yet I am not the forest you know about
although you might catch me at the farmer's market
in some little po-dunk town, where you least expect it,
gently touching each peach to find the one I want
with juice dripping down my giggling chin
you likely won't recognize me like this

You must have mistaken me for someplace else
I am not a strip mall with infinite choices
I don't offer long-term leases with slide up doors
I won't be offering anything on sale anytime soon
I am not imported or deported, and my size
is too enormous for any department except the Divine
you won't find me
hanging out with straw-sucking slurpies
and if I did pop in for some rhinestone earrings,
you wouldn't know it was me, my stilettos are blinding

You must have mistaken me for someplace else
I am not city sidewalks trampled under mindless soles

You can't write graffiti on my heart, the empty bottles

that rattle the night will not rattle my cagelessness

I am not the place of a crime scene, neither victim

or predator or something to be killed for

I am not late night windows glowing red or a speakeasy,

there is nothing easy about me, I am not barroom brawls

from gossiping glasses, but if I was, I would be the blues

You must have mistaken me for someplace else

I am not the new place to be

where all the cool kids hang out

sip wine with baby strollers and dogs in tow,

sunglasses aglow

I am not a side dish of ahi tuna tartar

with micro-greens and truffle oil consumed

with flair on an afternoon escape

I am not a five star hotel with organic satin sheets

to rumple and toss

I am not a passing fling from a dating thing

although if you were to look for me,

I may be a clue, curled up in a corner

with a cup of tea, on a couch under a gingko balboa tree

You must have mistaken me for someplace else

I am not a residence, inhabitance, place to set up shop

not the furniture, not the door,

and certainly, not the doormat
I am not a convenience, Cuisinart,
or homemaker making home
I am not the place to work out the past. Sorry, no can do,
I might be open to working out the future with you
I am not any archetype you know of.
Not from anywhere around here

If I was anything near here, I would be the windows
where the hot morning light burns
white dotted curtains onto naked shoulders
I might not know what I was made for.
Likely to write this poem
I do know what I am made from,
starlight infused with blessings
composed of everything and nothing,
set to life by the One, yes, that One.
I have travelled a long way to get here,
yet I am not the universe

However, when you love me large enough,
I am the place the galaxies dance
as we follow the path of the sun
My milky breath and breasts,
the milky way, the only way to my heart
is to remember, you haven't been here before

Yet I might be the place you wish to call home,

and this, I am

We are not someplace we have ever been,

or ever will be again

The singularity of the day begs our attention

to time, space, place

Together we are journey and destination,

wounded and healer united in one rib

Invited to a place we create,

beyond black holes in wholeness

Are we are a cathedral of stars?

Are we a place to pray and play?

Are we perhaps the place we have been looking for,

all this time?

When I say, you must have mistaken me for someplace

else, I mean that who I am

is still a cooling sack of stardust in crucible of cowgirls

If you are looking for me, you will find me,

already in your arms

Yes, I am indeed, a piece of work.

And so are you. We should get along fine.

I have never been where you are, either.

Inspired by Milk and Honey Poems by Rupi Kaur

can you

Can you come from knowing
without making others feel
like they don't know
what you know?

Can you be in the presence
of other people's mistakes
without needing to bring them up
to show what you know?

Can you be intuitive
without looking too far
into other people's energy fields
especially without their consent?

Can you speak your truth
without needing to speak against
another
person's truth?

Can you be with the messiness
of a person's process
and see the beauty in it
without even the desire to clean it up?

unedited girl

The less
she edited
her full range
of emotions

the happier
and more colorful
she became

when people
asked her
how she got
so free

she took
them by the hand
and led them
into the
great mystery

"come with me, "
she said,
"you will see"

love dare

Let's pause and reflect on the power of love.

The power to make another person feel seen.

The gift of choosing to shine on our loved ones.

The courage to offer forgiveness to another.

The willingness to consider the barriers

we place against the love coming towards us from others.

So often we are caught up in right and wrong.

He said. She said. Who dun' it and who didn't.

Resistance. Righteousness.

Instead. Let's pause.

And reflect on the power of love.

I dare you to reach out to someone

that needs to hear from you

and tell them, I am sorry. I love you. I am right here.

Will you?

I will.

a mama day blessing

This day we honor and celebrate

the women who have given life to us

the women who give life to ideas

the women who died giving life

the women who wanted to have a child

but didn't get to

the women who right now

are tilling their fertile soil for new seed

This is for the women who choose

not to have a child but have many children

the women who are in captivity

the women who are free

those who were mothered well

and those who had crazy mamas

because any mama that did not love you well,

was not well enough

This is for the women who are struggling

this moment to care for their babies

and the women who right now

snuggle with little ones under feather comforters

for those whose mamas have gone on

and for those who are mamas to be

for women who miscarried precious life
and those who carried many

For single mamas who want their mate
and for married mamas who want to be seen and heard
for those who never
got to have a mama hold them
and for those mamas whose children
will not speak to them
for happy mamas and sad mamas

For birth mothers who chose to deliver
a child into another mother's arms
and the Great Mama of all,
and the Mama who gave birth to God
and most of all…
for all women and men
who are in need of re-mothering.

Note: this one was written long ago but never go published in the other book so it snuck in here without my looking.

for those who are obsessed

Those who are obsessed with silence
Will find their days filled with incessant noise
When we can hear the symphony in chaos,
the fugue of existence
will invite us to be one of the players

Those who are obsessed with perfection and order
Will be hard pressed to collaborate with anyone
Especially the wildly expressed,
who may not have order as a value
Let those who desire order,
and those who are in chaos, dance

Those who are obsessed with their self-image
will find envy at every turn,
and friendships will be challenged
Lovers will grow tired of reassurance and it will be
difficult to ever be enough,
without choosing to be enough as we are

Those who are obsessed with ceaseless self-medicating
Will find ordinary reality a bore, or worse,
a battle to be fought

There are many reasons to alter reality,

beyond that of coping

May we learn to discover pleasure where it lives,

in presence

Those obsessed with making everything on purpose

Will be so busy turning mistake and disaster

into karmic stories

We will likely miss the wolf at the door

and the boiled frog

Can we see what there is

without making it a game of blame?

Those obsessed with saving others

are often the quizzical cases

Hiding behind the desire to cure,

judgment may be lurking

Unbeknownst to ourselves,

we have been inflicting ideas on another

When we can love without the desire to convert,

true friendship arises

Those who are obsessed with living to the fullest

may find we are disappointed

with the mediocrity of laundry

All the mundane tasks are seen as

prevention from being
When the fullest-ness available,
is to inhabit being - or is it?

Those who are obsessed with thinking we are in a battle
will find the time to sharpen our sword has passed
The over-vigilance, while needed,
wearies even the warrior
May we sharpen for the work at hand,
and soften for love-making

Those who are obsessed with dying a certain way
may find themselves surprised
when things do not go as planned
Once again the great mystery
throws another loop in her knitting
Every death story will be different
than the one you need to tell

Those who are obsessed with control and are good at it,
will be challenged again and again by failure and frailty
until suffering from unplanned outcomes
alchemizes our direction
We hope our practice, at least,
has forged us into a strong guide

Those who are obsessed with getting to another place,
like heaven
Will find we spend too much time fearing another place,
like hell
When all the while the people on the streets
are sitting in circle singing,
We missed it, because we wanted so much to be
anywhere but here

Those who are obsessed with the healing journey
Will find there is indeed always something to heal
When, if ever, will it be time to leap
from the healing journey?
Declare, "It is enough, we are healed enough
for a new story!"

Those who are obsessed with the opiate of poetry
Will take strange comfort
in narrating the terrors of our times
Words will shake us from slumber
to wield the pen, or else!
As if it is the most important moment of our lives,
it might be
It might be, that simply showing up for the conversation
is enough for this life, this day, this minute, this second

The spell of being – being broken open in praise

gives us a chance

To experience being human

and glory is unveiled in us

Those who are obsessed with the light

Will find themselves dodging shadows

as if they are predators

Those who are overly obsessed with shadows

Will find there are many of us sitting beside

you holding the light

Those who are obsessed with sensitivity,

protection, shielding

Will find little comfort in the separation

from this current crisis

We feel it all anyway,

and in our resistance become cloaked

Does it matter if it is crisis or paradise

if we are made for this time?

Those who support systems that condemn justice for all

that rationalize the privatization

of water and food and medicine

Are hard to love, for those of us who value

our life here on earth

May we be brave enough to risk new friendships

across the imaginary lines

When those who are obsessed with blaming

can forgive ourselves and everyone,

including the Creator

Who we have been quietly blaming all along

for this plan gone awry

Then we can wake up to serve

in the crisis happening in our neighborhood

Those who are obsessed with avoiding

the suffering of others

Will find the suffering everywhere

an impossible barrier to joy

When we know that the paradox

is the supple threshold of ecstasy

Then we can hang on

and let go at the same time and be free

Those who are obsessed with calling circles

for everything and every occasion

will find we are very busy in these last days

dishing up meaning

Breaking bread and pouring out the wine,

while singing new and old songs

May praise be found on our lips

for all the goodness we have shared

And if in the end we rage instead of surrender,

so be it as long as we show up for that experience

And if in the beginning we find ourselves where we

started and know it newly, so be it

Let's not save our lives - let's live them

When we find the thing

that we would do if we had forever

is in harmony with the thing we would do

if we had only one day left

Then we have arrived, and we will be welcomed home

"We shall not cease from exploration, and the end of all our exploring will be to arrive where we started and know the place for the first time." ~ T.S. Eliot ~

formidable

When you opened the door
you saw her standing there
portfolio under her arm
blue eyes wide, starched pants and shirt
looking like the paper boy.
Finally you said:
Oh, you are an artist.
Come in.
From there you opened the world.
Art. Poetry. Spirit. Wood. Clay.
Stone. Bone. Woman. Idea. Spirit.
Formidable woman.
You gave her, what she gave me.
Tool of my hand
Language of my heart.
A way of working,
Working it out.
Shaping the stone of us.
You shape us still with
mighty tools, chipping away
to reveal the inner being.

For Lenore Thomas Straus

beauty walking

She is beauty
walking into the room
waking the room with her presence.

Silver hair in a love knot
Pearls long and lean
Small black dress just below the knee
Cowgirl boots in black
Lipstick red.
Commanding and yet supple.
Delighting the eye and heart,
making us all feel loved.

My mother is beautiful
and her eyes know all my worlds
Her words open all the doors
She stands by me and stands for me
and stands on her own.

She is beauty walking,
waking the room with her presence.
My mother is a poet
and she has taught us this seeing,
this being.

grown strong together

We have grown this together
in time and in work we have labored
Side by side with hands in mud,
glitter, tears, fears, cares and plenty
of red wine in big glasses
over conversations that stir the muse

We have grown this together
this kind of loving, this kind of thinking
this culture of creation where woman
is honored for all she is - all she isn't
is not our concern, we just lift her up!
This friendship is rooted in 'woman'

We have grown this together
sharing conversation late into the dark night
and early with the kittens and kind mornings
This does not mean everything has been said
We have grown up and on and so find
less of a need to call out wrong and right!

We have grown this together
an abundance of culture and community
shaping the cup of creativity with desire

and with the love of the stardust matriarch
and the poet mother muse
we question every establishment and ask the impossible

We are keeper of the flame of sisterhood
Cosmic Cowgirls, a tribe of wild ones who
straddle the world in wonder and inquiry
From the first gathering and the last you are woven
Courting conversation and query and
stringing beads along the red thread for over 300 calls

We have shared friends and long black coats,
even cowgirl boots with winged phoenix flying
We have prayed for lovers and cried for lovers
We have hung the show with wet paint over
and over and lit the candle of hope
for our countries, both lost in their way

We have grown strong together

For Mary MacDonald

for those who crave

For those who crave a lover
who will rock our worlds
May find that we must awaken our muse
And instead of lists and requirements
become the one
in whose space the rocking occurs

For the husbands who crave their wives
to give them space
For the wives who crave their husbands
will see them with new eyes
We have all been taught to ask
for what we think we want
What happens if you stop wanting
the thing you think you want?

For those who crave patterns and consistency
We will find ourselves interrupted
by adventure after adventure
Until we understand that the pattern is the interrupt
Then we can embrace the perfect storms coming our way

For those who crave release from this mortal coil
To know you are not alone in such a deep way

That the very fabric of our presence in loving you
Keeps you from the edge of your abyss

For those who crave to be famous or get found out
To wake up to what's truly needed
Which is to do our work and forget the rest
What if we trusted enough to let it happen, or not?

For those who crave a life other than what they have
Yet cannot conceive of changing what they have
May you find a space in your life to explore otherness
That does the least harm while you discover your way

For those who crave money
Will find they are never satisfied with enough
Enough has left the building already
Let us find something to crave that nourishes
what we truly need to live.

For those of us who crave to prove the existence of God
To the point where we are ravaged
with despair at separation
Understand that craving is a form of true connection

this revolution will not be ugly

This revolution will not be ugly.

We won't be degrading anyone in the process.

We will not justify cruelty in the cause.

We won't condone any violence in deed or word.

We will not use our rage as an excuse to insult others.

Any...others.

This revolution will not be about war-making.

We will not spend our energy fighting broken systems.

We will not compromise our health and wellness.

We will not turn the revolution into a profit- making
enterprise.

We will not blame our depression on others.

Any...others.

This revolution will be curated in beauty.

We will learn to say what we will do,

instead of just what we won't.

We choose to see ourselves and our part

in the unfolding story.

We will learn to transform 'fight' energy

into wisdom-led action.

We will name our own exile, and step into circles of
peers.

All...one.

This revolution will be a conscious revolution.

We are on a waking up journey –

we choose how we engage.

We will turn our fury into creativity,

dancing, poetry, and art.

We will practice curiosity

as a method of mindfulness.

We will serve those who are suffering,

in expanded ways.

We will continue our work,

as if our work mattered.

All...one.

This revolution will be led by peacemakers.

We will choose truth-tellers and edge-walkers

to guide us.

We will not wait to be guided

but guide ourselves from within.

We will step into our own authority

and make new patterns.

We can be a danger to the establishment

without self-harm.

All...of us who choose, will curate the revolution in

beauty.

do dream in gold: ode to fellow entrepreneurs

This wasn't easy
but you knew that
going in, or did you?

You didn't know
just how 'not easy'
discovering ease would be

You got up too early
stayed up too late -
still you felt behind

You bought too many URLS
while drinking a bottle of red wine alone
A business expense, of course

You forgive yourself for naming every idea
like it was new found gold
you felt it in your bones as truth

A hum humming idea
A ding dingalinging launch plan
A gold coin dropping into a cup

Now, don't get me wrong:
It is good to dream of gold
people with ideas and time, often do

If you have been looking for a sign
This is it: You are on a right path
Keep going towards your vitality
Oh, the astonishment of the steps!
The number of steps it takes to launch
To rise, the play, to be seen!

After the capture page, the funnel,
The bucket and then the f*ck it all,
If this is what it takes. (Does it?)

After some transformational coaching
On selfless service and self-love
You remembered why you did this

You have become enlightened
So you made a choice not to sell
To the pain point. Gold stars for you!

Yes, gold stars in your third eye
They say all that shimmers isn't gold
Some of us just love the shimmer

Every cliché has been pasted on
Your office wall to encourage you:
To Keep Going No Matter What

You show up and your best look
Is better on most days than most others.
You look good, right? I mean, right?

How much of this is about that,
Looking good? Selling success?
Continual re-evaluation is part of this plan.

The idea, the dream, the desire
May have been reduced to logo stickers
you can stick on the side of cups or cars

Yet, don't doubt for a second
You did have to do it.
It was yours to do!

No matter how it has turned out

The exploration was worth

the price of admission, and your savings

Do dream in gold dear ones,

Someone has to, it may as well be you

In that dreaming, remember you

Remember the real reason you started,

Opened that door and hung that shingle

Remember, it all counts, every single thing.

Especially you! So, the next time you have

a business appointment, bring a cake!

A party without a cake is just a meeting!

hidden self

Say to your hidden self:

"I am sorry.

I didn't know you were in here.

I am here now.

I didn't know how to speak to you.

I am willing to learn your language.

Show me the ways.

I don't know how to approach you.

Yet I will try...in the humble desire of becoming.

Let me be supple in my invitations."

Say to your hidden self:

(as if looking into the eyes of one you love)

"I love you, even without knowing you, really.

Yet I have always known you...somehow.

May these words be an offering on your altar.

I am here now. I know I didn't listen.

I know it was a long ride home.

Please. Forgive me. I am ready to show up.

I wasn't taught how to think about you.

Let alone that it was okay to feel how I feel.

Now that I know that you are here - I am at home."

Say to your hidden self:

(as if you are speaking to a child you knew, now grown)

"When I was yet a little one, we talked and played.

Now that I am grown, I hope we can talk and play again!

I want to know what I have been hiding from myself!

I have no interest in being asleep to you!

I trust that all the stories I have already lived

can be useful preparation for this encounter.

You are so much bigger since the last time I saw you.

You are beautiful. I have missed you. Would you join me

for a cup of tea? We have so much to talk about..."

Say to your hidden self

(now more revealed...)

"I have been waiting for you. I see your edges ripple.

I shall wait no more, but be here, where you are.

Show me, dearest soul, how to live as myself."

whispering to hurricanes

I am witnessing you.
Watching, tending, caring for you
and your path, in any way I know how.
I am sending love to
those who are afraid and hurt
while still loving you and
all of the earth and the elements.
Great respect.
I know this isn't a punishment or an intent to harm.
I know you are as strong and natural
as you understand yourself to be.
And still, we here, the children of earth,
pray together with one voice
for the peace at the eye of your storm
to spread out and dissolve into loving.
We are paying attention.
Sending calm. Seeing beauty.

Jesus stood up and
commanded the wind
and said to the waves,
"Quiet! Be still!"
Then the wind stopped,
and it became completely calm.

How do you truly BE

WITH the great unfolding?

When you see and

hear of devastation,

destruction and despair

experienced by others.

What do you DO? How do you be?

Just notice. Do you have a way of being?

Chosen or default?

Do you shut down?

Go quiet? Get angry?

Get obsessive?

Start praying like wild?

With the elements shaking things up

around the world,

the earthquake in Mexico last night

and the Hurricane hurling towards Cuba,

Florida today, and everything

that has happened in the US since

Charlottesville. We are certainly

in a wake-up call, I feel.

And waking up is often

hard before it is good.

What stories are you making up

about what is happening?

I anthropomorphize tragedy

at times to get in touch with it

and so do the hurricane people by naming it in gender.

Some turn to prophecy to explain

what's happening and our eventual

destruction – others turn to climate change

and shaming. Some say the earth is angry.

Others say God is angry.

I don't think of it like that at all.

I also feel the blame game can keep us from feeling.

I say, let's feel first. And then go from there.

In our feeling, we can be in contact

with our soul space,

which is the only place we can protect from harm,

and the best place to live from,

in my view. And the thing that will best empower us

on behalf of others.

My Red Thread Letters are about

encouragement for the journey

so, I am encouraging you to get conscious

about how you are with what's happening around us.

That's it.

Get conscious and know how you are –

so that you can choose

how you are going to show up.

If we who are strong allow ourselves to be
disempowered,
how than can we serve?
Can you choose not to turn from suffering
and yet not obsess to the point of no return?
(I ask you and myself this)
I will not go to sleep on the questions love asks.
Against all odds, let us pray.
What else are you going to do?
Do you have any part of it to manage within yourself?
Can you manage yourself enough to begin
to bring that compassion out to others and
yes, to Irma, herself?
Who will we become by practicing
a loving we do not understand but
long to be united with?
We will become more empowered
to do good than if we didn't.
So, let's show up first with feeling and
consciousness and then act.
Let's talk about water and intention.
We know, that water, changes when we speak to it.

We live in a responsive universe.
This is NOT an idea of the woo woo world.
This is science – how then can we engage

with it in a mighty way through our thoughts?

It changes and

THEN WE ARE CHANGED

THROUGH WITNESSING IT.

Feeling brave?

Get a bowl of water, speak to it,

speak to the oceans and lakes and the water

being used to put out the fires

and the water in the hurricane.

Offer it to the earth. Be present.

Your presence is enough and is needed.

As for me and my house,

we are whispering to water.

Not screaming, and adding to fury.

Whispering, loving.

Listening to her story.

However this works, there is a mythos unfolding

right now on planet earth.

To the hurricane,

I contribute my tears of calm

and my love that it will begin now

to lessen the force and

return to the sea and dissolve.

I speak to the un-spiraling of the momentum.

I am not just asking for prayers without thinking

about what that would really be like

at the level of science

and matter and molecule and…

I am seeing it lessen and asking my community

and circles to see that with me.

I am speaking prayers of quantum physics

across the stormy seas.

Join me in whispering to hurricanes

if you choose. Amen.

You can also alternate between fire and water,

as the United States is seeing some of

the worst fires on record –

it is hard to know where to focus

one's energy so I am just alternating –

I often put fire and water in one painting –

even the Lady above has both.

Today I am just focusing on this water

piece because of it being Her feast day.

Consider spending time honoring fire and water as a part

of your process.

Does praying do any good?

In dialogue about these disasters,

people are adding prayers,

then someone shames them,

as if it does no good.

Does anyone not know about how love travels?

How bio-photons can move to another person?

How about quantum entanglement?

Do you believe we are all connected?

Praying in hard times is normal,

even for those who don't feel connected by faith.

This praying we do

isn't about if it does any good.

We will never know – rather

it is about our conscious participation in creation.

And how we are changed through it,

becoming whole even in the fragmentation.

Which, if we consciously participated in co-creation,

perhaps we would know how to tend

this earth in a sacred manner.

We are being forced into seeing

how our ways must change. And really,

we don't know if 'we' as humans 'did' this.

Let's watch our stories of

punishment and reward.

There are other views, you know.

We can't know – so we can NOT blame

and yet still take responsibility to

create the future we want to be a part of creating.

A story of Yeshua, calming the storms.

So, in that mythos, we know it has been done.

Maybe it be so now, if it is possible

and for the highest good.

My counsel?

Call your mother and father.

Call your children.

Call those you love and

Say, "I am sorry.

I love you.

I am with you.

Let's be connected through all of this.

Together, we are stronger."

Clear your altar.

Bring fire and water to your altar.

Choose to be conscious and loving.

Pay attention.

Turn towards your own creativity

to stay clear and calm with yourself.

Mind your own house

and loved ones in a new and

potent ways.

Pray for clear seeing, clear being.

And finally, dance....

as if your dance itself was part

of the solution of everything.

How we choose to engage

shapes our capacity to engage.

Resiliency is learned through action.

I just called my beautiful mama, Caron,

We talked for an hour about prophecy

and the Holy Spirit and what the heck is going on.

We talked about the gender in religion,

about patriarchy, about end times.

We talked about the signs of the times,

and the man who ran into the fire at Burning Man.

We talked like we have always done,

since the time I was young,

about the attacks on humanity.

We wondered if we were already boiled frogs.

We laughed, cried, and I said,

"I don't know what to do Mama."

I can't just say,

PRAY TO GOD.

But I can, try, in my own way

to be a presence of the Holy Spirit, the Comforter.

Not to tell you what to think or do,

but share my story with you,

and invite you into co-creation.

Whatever else we can do –

we can choose to wake up,

and become conscious.

Without this, without awareness,

I don't really know where we can go together.

I want to say one more thing about water and faith.

Since the water that has become toxic

can be changed to be beautiful again through our

intention –

can we not together, with one mind, and heart,

change the tides of the direction we are spiraling?

I don't know, but I know trying makes me who I am.

I never write to you expecting agreement,

I write to encourage you to think your own thoughts

and hope mine can provoke

your own process in a beautiful way

Anything we love can be saved ~ Alice Walker

marking death

Marking death.

And so, it continues –

open fire on innocence.

Part of my practice

this year is full awake-ness –

which is a personal path for each person to define.

I wanted to share my process in case

it is helpful in your own processing.

Please feel free to share too –

and together we will learn resilience.

For me - marking death and injury in my own country

is part of my practice. Often I mark it

for other countries as well, since I track global events,

specifically impacting women and girls as my focus.

This is not a morbid practice.

Rather it is how I let myself feel –

without shutting down and stay engaged

with this Beloved humanity.

This kind of emotion plus physical action

moves energy and keeps it from getting stuck.

You will find your own way with this –

and I share my process as

inspiration and catalyst

for an awake people in an awakening world.

It is marking prayers.

It's saying - I see you - suffering –

and in this tiny way

I shall not turn my eyes or heart away.

I shall also mark victories and blessings,

of which there are so many more!

I hesitate to share this although,

I have before. I hesitate to include it in my curriculum.

And. Most of the women I serve –

serve others as Leaders or Healers,

or are moms, sisters, aunties and Grammies

who will need to answer to their young ones.

I have marked many kidnappings and deaths

and wars and miscarriages and in that I am saying –

"Yes, I am one with all that is our human family."

I will not go to sleep on the questions love asks.

Tell your loved ones today

what they mean to you.

Hold them close.

Forgive what you can.

Embrace your own precious heart.

Pray to Creator for wisdom if you are

open to deepening that relationship to the mystery.

This painting process is for a year and a day

to bring the whole story of the year into context –

this is on the edge of the canvas which is

painted black to hold space for the mystery –

the white is white light.

Then I bless it with holy water and myself.

Here's the flow - I paint it and as I am. –

I send my prayer out first to the harmed

and then the harming - and then my own Beloveds.

And then the world of all beings.

I give it to Creator, and in that, –

choose not to carry the pain physically –

but to let it flow through my field and out as pure love.

It's intentional alchemy.

Fort Lauderdale, Florida

5 dead. 9 injured. 1 misguided.

The parents of the misguided.

The people impacted on earth.

The earth with roots to lift this all up.

We are all works in progress.

The first message from my Muse

about this painting for a year is:

This is where the loving happens. Indeed.

#IMAGINE

cantos of reclamation

She is the quickening
Standing at the threshold of now

She doesn't perform alchemy
She is the embodied alchemical process

She doesn't need to create legacy by design
She IS the legacy, as it reveals itself

She certainly isn't waiting to be discovered
The Lady has already discovered herself!

She is not persuaded by readings of the almost future
That hold prophecies of prescribed delivery or doom

She carries the codes of the tree of life in her blood
She prays to be ready to receive the fullness of the
teachings

She need not constantly seek to heal what is wounded
She carries holy wholeness in her unbroken soul

With supple shimmer, she slips out of stories worn old
Gliding from hidden worlds into the joy of pure presence

She is woven of the 'matter' of mysterious darkness
A daughter of Wisdom, whose radiance never ceases

She is at the intersection where light enters the prism
Surrendering unnecessary struggle,
heralding an age of beauty

Her true lover is not her opposite, nor her reflection,
What they are, who they are, is still being in-formed

She is one of the many messengers of the ancient future
First re-membering, and then creating with intention

She is a shelter for the sacred, a call to action for the lost
The revealing of an archetype from the celestial eclipse

Her creativity, marks out the atlas of possibility
Dissolving duality, tending to reclamation and refuge

Where paths meet she takes her stand.
A vesica piscis view weaving technology
and biology as stardust methodology

She knows from whence the gifts come, from the Creator,
She chooses the narrow path of the one called The Way

The lineage she carries is carried by all people

Yet often lays hidden

under suppression of consciousness

She calls a council to gather, Mystics, Poets,

Painters, Cantors, Scientists, Dancers, Wisdom Keepers

and Christos Seekers

As an initiation they reclaim language, image, code,

seed and sound

A new mythos is revealed,

already carried in the codex of the soul

Together they explore the intersections

that have divided us

Offering up a view of generosity,

 prosperity and justice

She shrugs off continual apology for self

and projections from others

With acceptance and forgiveness for self and others,

she emerges

She steps out of systems of any kind

that do not support life

Simultaneously stepping into structures of divine design

She is the scribe and curator of her own becoming
Guided by her call to the ministry of refuge
and reclamation

She accepts with gravity,
her responsibility to the great unfolding
Nurturing herself, she discovers the nurturing
for those she serves

Her unreasonable prayer
is a song for the wellness of all
An offering of love, comfort
and an invitation to the quickening

She hopes that this reading may be a Blessing for you,
as it has been for Her, in the writing and the revelation.

The writing of one's own Cantos of Reclamation
can be a ritual towards the awakening.

Join me at the council and shelter for the sacred?
We will be there, waiting and ready to dance!

changing management

I am talking to you,
but I am talking to me.
To all of us. I am not the one in the know.
I am however, one of the torchbearers
willing to ask the questions.
Are you operating on the 'grid'
instead of the matrix?
Is your plan for your sacred work
aligned to nature?

Is the way you live your life linear and patterned –
or is it dynamic and resilient?
Have you ever considered building a business plan based
on sacred geometry instead of our current models?
Have you been practicing marketing 'techniques'
instead of following your own internal codes
for creating and sharing?

Are you working in harmony with the greatest powers
on the earth or against the natural flow?
Are you under the illusion that you can do it all yourself,
instead of aligning yourself
with sacred math and motion?
Do you think people are born leaders, or do they earn it?

Or discover it already within?
Do you, somewhere within you, know there
 is another way to work/be/experience,
that honors both the mystical and the scientific
Where there is not a conflict but TOTAL alignment?
Is your current belief system in need of an upgrade?

If your current belief system is based on out-moded
models of manifestation, attracting people
and things to you through self-will
and harnessing your own power to make things happen,
think again. Just. Think again.

Have you made assumption about how
the universe 'works' and yet haven't dipped your toe
into how it actually does work (as far as it has been
revealed)?

There MAY be something more you don't know yet,
about your own discovery journey and access to power
that these old beliefs may be blocking.
About your own gifts
and how to work with the universe. It
 may be different than you think,
but it is the most natural place in the world.

I'm not a leader, just a creature,

seeking the features of a teacher.

Whether you follow or whether you lead

All mysterious ways of nature and I'm into it.

Changing management.

And there are various ways to conquer this

monotonous metropolis, my stubbornness is bottomless,

my fearlessness is talking sh*t

and I'm wide awake and I'm taking names.

~ Nakho Bear ~ Aloha Ke Akua, Medicine for the People

"There is a vitality, a life force, a quickening that is translated through you into action, and there is only one of you in all time, this expression is unique, and if you block it, it will never exist through any other medium; and be lost. The world will not have it. It is not your business to determine how good it is, not how it compares with other expression. It is your business to keep it yours clearly and directly, to keep the channel open. You do not even have to believe in yourself or your work. You have to keep open and aware directly to the urges that motivate you. Keep the channel open. No artist is pleased. There is no satisfaction whatever at any time. There is on a queer, divine dissatisfaction, a blessed unrest that keeps us marching and makes us more alive than the others." ~ Martha Graham

god is not my girl friday

Things didn't turn out the way I hoped.

Most of my biggest prayers

did not turn out the way I prayed.

What I thought I wanted

wasn't what ended up happening.

So, does this mean God isn't listening?

No, it just means God is not my Girl Friday

taking dictation from my desires.

Did it turn out better than I hoped?

Well, in some cases yes and in some no,

but that really isn't the right question is it?

Getting what we think we want is perhaps

the wrong idea, often leading to disappointment.

My faith cannot be based on any results,

emotions expressed or dreams come true.

In gratitude I leave behind an idea that

when things are good I am in favor with the Divine.

And when I perceive that things are out of order,

it may be some kind of punishment for bad behavior.

Things here on earth and how it relates to the cosmos

certainly aren't even close to what we think.

Claiming we know how it works just isn't for me.

Consciousness is not the reward of hard work,

rather it is a deepening intimacy with the Beloved

that causes us to see in new ways.

Seeing what we haven't seen before

but has always been there.

This can be a beautiful path.

Yes, I do believe we contribute to the beauty through

our noticing of it and admiration of the Creator's

handiwork.

Thank God that God is not my errand boy

and does not spend time shaming me

for getting it right or wrong.

It isn't that I don't think God is here, real, and intimate.

I do. I count on it. My faith rests right there without

needing any more evidence than earth, air, fire, water,

and me being alive.

I wonder if the universe is having an experience

through us, as the Divine?

Most of the time I just ask questions these days

instead of making any requests at all.

Unless I am desperate, then I just beg.

Then I remember, I am made of stardust, soil and

Holy spit and everything falls into place as grace.

I still have no idea what is going on

and perhaps I have given up needing to know at all.

Saying I am a disciple of creation feels too lofty

but in my heart, I feel I am.

181

I shall spend my life in love with this place I find myself,

even and especially when I don't get what I think I what.

It is ok not to know what we want,

how it works, or why things happen the way we do.

There isn't a formula for it we aren't allowed to see yet.

We aren't ready to see what there is yet, glimpses

inspire poets, artists, musicians, dancers,

and dreamers to dream.

Somehow, not knowing

has become the relief of many ages.

Shedding skins and archetypes

and potential past lives.

Even exiting ideas like karma

or deserving or getting good at 'this.'

This is likely not a punishment and reward system

although that idea has propagated a lot of suffering

and good works in trading for paradise.

Answered prayer is not a reward,

although we may praise God.

Unanswered prayer is not a punishment,

although we may blame God.

Or ourselves. Feels almost as bad to do either one.

I will just try to praise no matter what.

Hands up, heart open,

paint brush ready to move prayers across canvas.

I don't want to trade for paradise.

I just hope to be awake when God comes

to the door of my heart.

I listen for the knock

like a baby listens for their mother's footsteps.

I choose to be an offering.

My life is an offering. Sometimes that means

there is sacrifice, and sometimes, mostly, blessings.

But that isn't because God sees to it that I see.

Rather, how I make myself available to God

is my sacred assignment embodied.

My natural state is to turn blessings into offerings,

encouragement for the journey for fellow travelers.

I want to do my part. I think I am. I don't know.

I just know when I create, I feel part of creation.

For you created my inmost being,
you knit me together in my mother's womb.
I praise you because I am wonderfully made,
your works are wonderful,
I know that full well. ~Psalm 139~

vigil

Let us light a fire in our hearts

holding vigil for Virginia and all

the people connected to the story.

Which is all of us.

Let us not go to sleep on the questions

love asks.

Invite your friends and family

to talk about how this feels for them.

What is coming up for them? For you?

We need to be in conversation.

Conversation will help us

not go to sleep and navigate

the future together.

Holding vigil with you, my sisters

and brothers, who honor one another,

who cherish diversity,

who respect humanity

and who do no harm.

In the beginning God created the heavens and the
earth. Now the earth was formless and empty,
darkness was over the surface of the deep, and the
Spirit of God was hovering over the waters.
~ Genesis 1:1 ~

delicious darkness

morning's soft dark velvet

slips across the sill

whispers in my ear:

"this is your time "

the delicious darkness

of the first hour

before the song of birds

before the rustling leaves

before the events of the day

before dressing

the real work is working

rise slowly without a sound

light a single candle and sit still

watch the light move

the tangerine tinting

the palest blue rising

as the aqua night

becomes a new self,

you too have a chance

to become new

will you?

this very morning

has called you from slumber

because it has a poem

waiting for you

drenched in memory shooting stars

we all know how busy you can be

and so we made this morning

for you

words float from my fingertips

they had been waiting for me

to become available

neither rushing or restless

they soothe the aching places

in the delicious darkness

of this first hour which

I now know will belong to me

from this moment on.

tears fall without cause

I say to the morning

"Hello, and Thank you.

I am here"

held

I hold this earth in my heart.

I hold this fire in my heart.

I hold all the waters in my heart.

I hold this cosmos in my heart.

I hold all of you - every single one of you in my heart.

Especially those who know me.

Especially those who do not know me.

Everything is made sacred in the heart.

I wish that a temple be erected here quickly, so I may therein
exhibit and give all my love, compassion, help, and protection,
because I am your merciful mother, to you, and to all the
inhabitants on this land and all the rest who love me, invoke
and confide in me; listen there to their lamentations, and
remedy all their miseries, afflictions and sorrows.

Hear me and understand well, my little son, that nothing
should frighten or grieve you. Let not your heart be disturbed.
Do not fear that sickness, nor any other sickness or anguish.
Am I not here, who is your Mother? Are you not under my
protection? Am I not your health? Are you not happily within
my fold? What else do you wish?
~ 1531 spoken to Jaun Diego by La Virgin de Guadalupe ~

i crave the quickening

There are days when you realize
that who you were is no longer who you are.
This could be a curiosity or a cause for grieving.
When we wake up, sometimes there is anger
at having been sleeping so long.
I get it. I really do.

Most of us have felt this way on one day or another.
Roll around on the ground for a while
hugging your knees to your chest
and wailing poetic distress if you must, then, get up!
We have work to do -and- you may be late,
or, perhaps right on time.

Today I am weaving with the lightning
of the gatekeepers who keep the gates of my circles.
Their threads are woven of the elements of course,
Earth, Air, Fire, Water, Ether and Shimmer
My hands, no longer as quick as they once were,
are eager to see just what we might have made together.

Something I have never seen before emerges
as our common past threads create the fabric
for the uncommon future. Something

that wasn't going to happen unless you showed up.

Yes. You. You there. The woman I saw
in the darkening lamplight at the red thread café that
night.
That was before now, before the quest.
Before all visionary visions and late- night teas
with my midnight muse or yours
in the alchemy of soul fire.
A restless one, aren't ya? Ah. Me too.

It's been quite a journey now hasn't it?
We have been traveling forever to get here, haven't we?
There is a quickening now because of you.
I can feel it moving like a storm brewing over water.
Rumbling. Humbling. Humming. Stirring the deep.
I sense that these gatekeepers are dangerous
in the best possible way.
They make me shake in my boots. Quaking to presence.

Tremble, oh ye world of sleepers.
The wakened women have come
to rattle the windows of the soul
with paintbrushes filled
with gold paint and stardust. Keep Watch!
Latch your doors if you desire to keep the sleep.

Things will never be the same again.

Those of us who have been waiting for this day

will do a jig in magenta boots

with magic capes of scarlet

painted with poetry in a foreign tongue.

This isn't a private party. But.

There is an initiation.

What's that you say –

what will be required if you attend?

Well the quickening of course.

You have to agree to be quickened.

Which is a riddle only the initiates can ask you.

Don't ask me the passwords.

I am only the weaver and the maker of the tea.

I joined this circle because I crave the quickening.

Dedicated to the Color of Woman Class of 2016

say to your hidden self

Say to your hidden self:

I am sorry.
I didn't know you were in here.
After all, you are…hidden.

I am here now.
I didn't know, how to speak to you.
I am willing to learn your language.

I don't know how to approach you.
Yet I will try, in earnest desire.
I have always sensed you, I think?

Say to your hidden self:

I love you, even without knowing you, really.
Yet I have always known you…somehow.
Let these words be an offering on your altar.

I am here now.
I know it was a long ride home.
Please. Forgive me. I am here now.

I wasn't taught how to think.

Let alone that it was okay, to feel, how I feel.

Yet now that I know that you are here, I feel at home.

Say to your hidden self:

When I was yet a little one, we talked and played.

Now that I am grown, I hope we can talk and play.

I want to know what I have been hiding from myself!

I have no interest in being asleep to you!

Who I have been, is in preparation for this encounter.

Will you help me rise, to waking?

Say to your hidden self:

As if you would say to a child now grown.

You are so much bigger since the last time I saw you.

You are beautiful. I have missed you. I am here now.

highway to you

My Love ~

What I want you to know:
Today as we drove through the hills
I loved you more than any other day
Sometimes you ask me if it's really true
Oh babe, it is as true as I know to be.

Everything was tender
A field of cows laying down
With baby cows, black and white
Made me tear up and I reached for you.

As we wandered care-free
Along the Carneros Highway
The place we live, together,
The HWY2U and me is beautiful.

I thought to write this not 2 U
About what I want you to know.
I want you to know this: I love you.
That is why I said, and do say: I DO.

I am happy
As happy as I have ever been
Or expect to ever be
My HWY2U is a happy one!

I wake up to talk to you
I find myself missing you
Though you are just in the other room
I call to you in the night.

I want you to know
If anything happens to me
That I was, I am happy
That what you showed me, was good.

The healing that happened
In the landscape of my soul
The year you came,
Changed everything.

If anything goes wrong
From this moment onward
Let it be known by you
That I am yours.

All yours.

The pleasure, the possibility,
is where I live in you
Your embrace, my home.

So, in any moment
When you might wonder
Or your mind or heart might wander
I am here.

When you came home, a year ago...
You patted your shoulder and said.
This is your home.
I moved in.

So, I want you to know,
I am here, and will be here
Your love has changed
The landscape of the world I live inside of.

There are SO many more things to say
If one considers what one might say
If they were no longer here
The clues from every action are reviewed

So, most of all

Most important of all

Is this: I choose you.

KNOW that YOU are CHOSEN by me.

I am always on a HWY 2 U

My precious one

Have always been

On a HWY 2 U

sky on your skin

With sky on your skin

Pray outside at night

Walk out with your rattle or drum

Sound will clear a safe path

Wear as little as possible

Feel ancient star light on your skin

Lift your head up in awe

Stars will scatter signs on your face

Inhale the goodness of the earth

Medicine goes into your bones

Surrender yourself into the cloak of darkness

Receive the sensation of belonging here

Listen to the sounds of night settling

Stand unafraid at the threshold and begin

Chant everything that comes forward

Every living thing is chanting with you

Return what you have received

Night has been listening for you to come

behold

Today

Walk to the edge of yourself

See a door you have never seen before.

Don't knock.

Don't ask if anyone is home.

Just behold access.

Then without further consideration,

Dive in.

Once inside ask:

Who lives in here?

If it is silent,

Enjoy the strange break from all the voices,

for once they may not know what to say.

If it is filled with suggestions and tirades

kindly ask again.

Who lives in here?

(This is sacred space.)

It isn't about the answer of course.

This is about what happens in the act

of asking in earnest, about the real you.

Something not enough of us really do.

Your cooling sack of stardust is inhabited

but by who?

Not knowing what to do

or who to be next

is something we all experience.

Sometimes revelation visits this space.

Pay attention when that happens.

The important thing to know is:

There are many doorways

and you have access.

Go on in.

Today

walk to the edge of yourself

See a door you have never seen before.

Dive in. Behold, and ask

Who lives in here?

'Who lives in here?' ~ is a sentence inspired by my teacher, Sue Hoya Sellars. It is a sentence she always asked us to ask and included in her paintings – and the phrase cooling sacks of stardust is also her direct quote about identity.

change

Change your story
Change your life

Change your life
Change your worldview

Change your worldview
Change your community

Change your community
Change the future

Changing your mind
Changes everything

Change your story
Change your life

Change your life
Change your worldview

Change your worldview
Change your community

Change your community
Change the future

Changing your mind
Changes everything

barbies in a rockband

Washcloth comforters, white

Soup pot swimming pool, silver

Salad bowl hot tub, yellow

Mama's stiletto convertible, red

Shoebox single beds

Sox sleeping bags, polka dots

Ocean bathtubs with bubbles

Stuffed animal panther jungle cat, leopard

Stuffed animal horse for cowgirls, hot pink

House plant safari trips

Schoolbook stages for performance

Yes my Barbies were in a rockband

Forks for Guitars

Chopsticks for microphones

Bootbox double bed lovers

Bed lined with cashmere sweater, creme

Happily ever after

since i didn't become a mother

Since I didn't become a mother
There won't be any weddings
to attend where I see my child
on their special day.

There will be no tiny hands
held in these artists hands.
No grand-mothering on Sunday
while my children, now parents,
are on a date break from kiddos.
No pie recipes to teach
with a stick of warm butter and brown sugar
rolled together in soft and tiny hands.

No passing on of my own grandmother's scissors
Those scissors that have cut thousands
of red threads in hundreds of circles.

You can tell me I am mother to many and
indeed, it has been spoken, and I have heard you.
You can tell me my work will live on,
my life matters, I did my part.
And yes, I feel I have.

i was there - from my muse

I was with you when you prayed
laying on the grass as a girl.
This was our first altar.

I was with you, wielding the pen when
your earliest poetry revealed.
Yes, darling, the system is broken.

I was in the blood of the clay bowl
you shaped in the form of a woman.
You knew me then.

I was the one who called you
to the mountain to free your mind.
And your art. You didn't know my name.

I was the one who held your brush
to the canvas when you wanted to give up.
Then finally, slowly you saw who you are.

I was there at breakfast with you and him,
when the gaze he gave you showed you the truth.
Then we moved away. Mine were the wings.

I was there in the poetry readings in San Francisco
when you discovered you were more like a poet.
And less like a business executive.

I was there too in the early feminist rage,
and yes, was the one, to help burn it off into passion.
Love is me. I am love - large and in motion.

I have been here, prodding you along, forging
a path out of no path because I know the need.
The needs we two can conjure and feed.

I was there today, imagining with you
wild women set free in the sacred dance.
Brushes on fire for transformation.

I am in your cup of tea, your red thread café,
Your yesterday and tomorrow.
I am here, let's play!

this day by jonathan mccloud

I listened to our mountain waking.
Wrapped in her cloak of rest amongst inky silks
She has made off into the night
taking my weariness.
Leaving me to the places and spaces that I will be from
when she returns for me.

She reaches for me through the open window.
Her fingers pale and velveteen.
Green gray caresses as soft as mother's love
she whispers to me with mercies and promise.

In that which is the first moment
the darkness of slumber relaxes its grips.
Receding and dancing with the pale light she returns
easing on the color, tints and contrast
foretelling of the Sun's love and hot coffee.

Listening is a wonderful way.
The all-too-soon has arrived.
The light will reveal, steal and render
my sleeping mother awake.

The sounds of her respiring quietly
gentle and soft in her rhythms
here on the dark side of her garments
encourage my eyes to stay closed.
They beg me still and silent for a few more moments
to hear and to learn from her transformation.

I shall use more stillness this day.

~ *A morning at Terra Sophia. Autumn 2017*

*I wanted to include this from my love – to honor him in my
journey and to share his poetry with you, dear reader.*

about shiloh sophia

At the age of 24, Shiloh Sophia left the corporate world of art, education and business behind and a year later had her first of many sold out shows. She is a renaissance woman of many mediums ~ painter, poet, curator, speaker, philosopher and co-founder of the worldwide movement of Intentional Creativity®,

"As a student, I discovered I wasn't a talented artist in the traditional sense. I had to find the images within and the messages they held. Once I did, nothing could stop my Muse from her mission. She chose to be a danger to the establishment, a rebel with a cause and creativity as here way to bring transformation to the world"

Shiloh also created her first million dollars in art sales before the age of 40. Today she continues to sell original paintings, as well as a wholesale line of cards, coloring books and art that has now been featured in over 300 specialty stores. However, her primary work is focused in teaching others to access creativity for themselves.

She achieved her success through empowering herself and those she serves through the teachings and lineage of Intentional Creativity. This form of creativity is an intuitive process that accesses internal imagery through story, inquiry and language connected with the heart. *"Creating with mindfulness is practiced wordwide, and always has been. We are simply bringing awareness to it in new ways and offering ways to practice it more consciously"*

Through art, music, dance, writing and ritual, Shiloh serves an ever- expanding group of thousands of students, both women and men, advocates in their own lives, who live in the Americas and regions around the world. Today these students are learning to expand their own consciousness into local and global communities through the use of Intentional Creativity and serve their Beloveds.

"Art opens the hidden rooms of our souls, where we will often find our authentic selves just waiting there for us," outlines Sophia. *"From here we can find our truest voice and speak from the soul."*

With an enduring influence that started in the 1930s, Shiloh's specific Intentional Creativity lineage began with New Deal WPA. (Works Progress Administration in the U.S.) artist, Lenore Thomas Straus. It's here the Zen concept of being still and owning the spark of creation to create through our own life's stories could be shared with the world. Working with Eleanor Roosevelt on several large public WPA sculpture projects, Straus was also the legal guardian for Shiloh's art mentor Sue Hoya Sellars.

Pivotal in the development of Shiloh's talents is poet, writer, illustrator and teacher is Caron McCloud, Shiloh's mother, who encouraged Shiloh from a young age to learn to create art and recite poetry. Caron also shaped Shiloh's ideas about how to show up in the world and to be original at all costs. Caron's mother, Eden, was also an artist, as well as her father, Gene.

"My mama taught me to expand my mind and heart from the time I can remember, showing me art, reading me poetry, and talking to me and listening to me, as if I had something to say. Turns out, I did. My grandmother Eden, was also a writer, painter, expert needlepoint artist and seamstress, so this runs in the family. My mom used to make drawings for me to color, and what was my first offering?: A coloring book! I grew up immersed into two creative studios, my mother and grandmother's dress making shop, hence the focus on threads and Sue and my aunt Janet's pottery studio, hence the fascination with the image of the feminine in form,"

Decades later with the working members of her growing community of Cosmic Cowgirls, including Mary MacDonald and Jenafer Owen, Intentional Creativity work was brought to the next level. It was then that a special teacher training initiative called the 'Color of Woman School' introduced itself in 2010. It was an exciting moment when certification to become a teacher with the Intentional Creativity Method began and this has continued with each year finding a full training for this 9 month vision quest.

As this training continues, over 250 Intentional Creativity teachers will offer education in special venues include prisons, hospitals, social services, boardrooms, schools and veteran services locations. Classes will also be held in numerous diverse locations including cruise ships, wine bars, yoga studios, concert halls, churches, retreat centers, homes and much more. Shiloh also teaches at universities and the United Nations offering her methodology as a way to transform trauma.

"I love serving those who serve as a primary directive. I think of life is a great adventure. This framework of creativity as 'intentional' has guided my path for over twenty-five years. Making our art through Intentional Creativity changes how

the art impacts us and how it, and we live in the world"

Using the ancient of the teachings of the Red Thread, which can be found in a many religious and spiritual beliefs from around the world, Shiloh believes in the connection of the Red Thread.

"That those of us who are destined to meet are always and ever moving toward one another. If you pause with me and connect in the quantum way, can you feel my love extending all the way to you in this non-time based moment? It is here. It is real. And we can teach it and share it: Easily. If we choose to show up for it, but I will teach you more about that when we gather!"

Shiloh Sophia has lives and works with her innovative poet and chef husband, Jonathan McCloud and their two kitties, Frida and Diego with their school and not-for-profit, Musea Sophia : The Intentional Creativity Foundation.

"We can choose be a part of the weave or we can sit by and let it unravel before our eyes. As for me, I am a weaver who calls others to gather their own threads and get to work. Each of us has our own sacred assignment to fulfill."

books and collaborations with the author

Color of Woman
She Moves To Her Own Rhythm
Her Evolution
She Dances Between the Worlds
On A Wing and A Dream
Heart Wings
Heart of the Visionary – Collaboration with Cosmic Cowgirls

Collaborations with Illustrations and Writings

Mending Invisible Wings – Illustrations, Cover Art and Writing with Author Mary Burgess
Hard Times Require Furious Dancing – Illustrator with Author
Alice Walker
Mother Mary Oracle – Illustrator with Author Alana Fairchild
The New Feminine Evolutionary, cover art and article
Untamed Heart – Intentional Creativity Collaboration
Peak Vitality – Cover art and article
Rachels Bag – Introduction, Cover Art and Illustrations with Caron McCloud

In Progress

Soul Fire Oracle Deck
Black Madonna Oracle Deck
Way of the Red Thread

Products www.shilohsophiashop.com
Shiloh's website www.shilohsophia.com
Projects www.intentionalcreativityfoundation.org
Community and Classes www.cosmiccowgirls.com
Training www.colorofwomanschool.com

honoring art ancestors

These words were all written in the spirit of what I teach called Intentional Creativity. Intentional Creativity has art ancestors the world over, as all ancient peoples created some kind of art with mindful intention. Whether that be for usefulness, beauty or story. They brought their consciousness into their art.

In our specific story of Intentional Creativity, we have a lineage of women who practiced this mindfulness in a specific way. Lenore Thomas Straus (1909-1988) who worked with the Roosevelt Family on giant stone sculptures articulating ideas like - what does the Preamble to the Constitution look like in stone? And then carved it. Lenore was the guardian and mentor of Sue Hoya Sellars (1936-2014), my teacher.

Sue would go on to inform the work of all the women in our family starting in the mid-sixties. I was born in 1970, so her influence was well woven into our lives by the time I came onto the scene. Most of the women in my family are artists and teachers in our own right, however, influenced by Sue in immeasurable ways about our approach to working. Whether that was working in clay or paint, or working on the land with the animals. My cousin, Bridget founded a Montessori School; my aunt, Jane is a sculptor, potter and runs a women's Tai Chi School; my sister, Shannon is a writer, advocate and in the music business; and my mother, Caron, is a poet, designer, painter and teacher. All of us in service to art, creativity and advocacy in some way. Each of us having students, each of us becoming teachers and guides to support others on their path. I would go on to create a school to certify teachers in Intentional Creativity, called Color of Woman, named after my first book and first gallery.

Our family connection with Sue goes further back in an interesting weave of fate - as before we ever met Sue, she studied at the College of Marin. My grandmother on my father's side, Helen, gave Sue continual enrollment in the pottery program. For years. Sue credited my grandmother with giving her a space to work and develop her own work. After I was born, Sue would discover the woman who was my grandmother was the same woman who had served her in her time of need. Many ancestral layers to reveal.

In my early twenties I embarked on a major mentorship with Sue that started with a year, and continues to this day. She would teach me what Lenore taught her- to bring the deepest prayer into our work. In my case, I would bring the ideas of Intentional Creativity to hundreds of thousands of people in my career as an artist and a teacher. Indeed, a return to an idea, whose time has come again. In my mentorship we worked with clay, wood, metal, pen and ink, and paint. She would invite me to bring my prayers into whatever I was working on - and to believe it was going out into the world towards my intention. Hence, the birth of Intentional Creativity on the land in Mendocino our family still stewards to this day.

Sue was a fine artist, in that she studied painting. I would not do as well as she hoped in my skill, yet I had what she called 'a way of working'. She often laughed that my style of painting was 'drive by painting' - too quick and cavalier for her chop wood, carry water approach to making art. Of course, there is always the regret that I didn't study with her more in art, but then there is the celebration that we taught together for over 15 years, serving women in our community of Cosmic Cowgirls. And deeply developing the language and understand of art as a tool for consciousness.

Since Sue passed walked on in 2014, my husband Jonathan and I have been on an excavation journey to discover more about Sue and her way of working and a deepened interest in the impact Lenore had. In 2015, we traveled to Maryland to the Greenbelt Museum to see Lenore's show. A piece of my art was included, as well as a piece by Sue, to demonstrate what the Greenbelt Museum calls, 'enduring influence.'

Today I got the gift of speaking to Lenore's daughter, Nora, and learned of her love of Sue. Lenore became the guardian of Sue as a teen, rescuing her from severe poverty and hardship, and bringing her into a life of studying art, philosophy, literature, music and culture - and Sue would earn her way through being the babysitter. Nora said that she adored Sue, and was very protective of her and good with children. She was devastated when Sue left for San Francisco. Each clue feels like a blessing. Another thread in the weaving of this great work I am called to and that I call others to as well. I was so glad to hear that Nora, had a few of Sue's pieces.

In my research, I came across this excerpt from renowned author, Doris Grumbach, when she came across a quote by Lenore in a book at a friend's house in Maine.

I am back at work culling material for this memoir from my notebook of last summer. At Peggy Danielson's house in East Blue Hill, where I tried to bury all thoughts of my seventieth birthday, I found a prayer the sculptor Lenore Thomas Straus had use to conclude her book on the process of creating a stone statue, now standing in Norway:

'O God,
hold my hand
that
holds the tool'

Without using those precise words, I often find myself praying similarly before I sit down with my clipboard. Substitute "pen" for "tool."

Peggy told me that in the last few days of Lenore's life, when she was dying of cancer, she worked on tiny wax sculptures. Much reduced in size from her customary larger-than-life heads, these little figures contrasted significantly with her heroic stones, signifying not just the diminution in her energies but her sense of how little was left to her life. Never once, having been compelled almost to give up her hold on life, did she abandon her art.

I share this with you today, as part of my own ongoing journey to explore legacy, my part in preserving it and my responsibility to it. As I ponder this, I think I could spend a lifetime researching this and I have my own art to make...should I not be focusing on that more? And my answer is there, right there. Through exploring the art ancestors that made it possible for me to do this work, I am indeed deepening in my own art and my capacity to tend it in sacred manner. I rather fancy the idea of creating a Museum of Intentional Art. One must consider the ideas that light up the soul, and this does. Intentional Creating is the most potent practice I have seen to awaken consciousness. And by all means, let us proceed to wake up.

Sue and Lenore both passed at the age of 78, creating art up into the very last second. They were so identified with their art that it was the center point of every relationship. I hope I live long enough to bring my great work out, and to honor these mighty women and my mother, Caron McCloud. I am so grateful to have had these women as my teachers and know that I would not be where I am today without their work - their dedication, suffering and the beauty they bring forth in their creations.

There is still much to be written and created about in regards to Intentional Creativity - and I am at the easel and workbench continually in that ecstatic struggle to create what is possible. To be the tool itself, used by Creator.

Creating with intentional symbolism to communicate and tell story is ancient and pervasive the world over. From the Red Hand Cave paintings of Aboriginal peoples of Australia, the Japanese Tea Ceremony, Egyptian glyph and myths, Russian icons coded with story and symbol, Shaman drums painted with personal medicine, sacred theater in Ancient Greece, Black Madonna rituals like the Sous Terre in Chartres Cathedral, skin story tattoos of the Hawaiian Islands, Native American beadwork, baskets and garments, Taize Musical Workshop from France, African dances for birth and death, to the modern movement of intuitive art being globally practiced – the references are truly everywhere and endless and in every culture in the world. We find this common red thread of creating to tell story extremely exciting and inspirational. And an invitation for people to draw ever nearer to creating with mindfulness in our lives.

May I, like Lenore, and Sue, remember to request, that a force greater than I understand, hold my hand as I hold the tools that shape the future.

May you find the prayer for your own 'way of working' that nourishes your soul.

~ shiloh sophia ~

Does not wisdom call out?

Does not understanding raise her voice?

At the highest point along the way,

where the paths meet, she takes her stand

beside the gate leading into the city,

at the entrance, she cries aloud:

"To you, O people, I call out:

I raise my voice to all humankind..."

~ Proverbs 8 ~

Hold on to what is good,

Even if it's a handful of earth.

Hold on to what you believe,

Even if it's a tree that stands by itself.

Hold on to what you must do,

Even if it's a long way from here.

Hold on to your life,

Even if it's easier to let go.

Hold on to my hand,

Even if someday I'll be gone away from you.

~ Pueblo Prayer ~

May love be at the center of all choices

~ Shiloh Sophia ~

Made in the USA
San Bernardino, CA
04 December 2018